AUTOMATED VEHICLES ARE PROBABLY LEGAL IN THE UNITED STATES

Bryant Walker Smith

November 1, 2012

Table of Contents

1 Executive Summary

This paper provides the most comprehensive discussion to date of whether so-called automated, autonomous, self-driving, or driverless vehicles can be lawfully sold and used on public roads in the United States. The short answer is that the computer direction of a motor vehicle's steering, braking, and accelerating without real-time human input is probably legal. The long answer, which follows, provides a foundation for tailoring regulations and understanding liability issues related to these vehicles.

The paper's largely descriptive analysis, which begins with the principle that everything is permitted unless prohibited, covers three key legal regimes: the 1949 Geneva Convention on Road Traffic, regulations enacted by the National Highway Traffic Safety Administration (NHTSA), and the vehicle codes of all fifty US states.

The Geneva Convention, to which the United States is a party, probably does not prohibit automated driving. The treaty promotes road safety by establishing uniform rules, one of which requires every vehicle or combination thereof to have a driver who is "at all times ... able to control" it. However, this requirement is likely satisfied if a human is able to intervene in the automated vehicle's operation.

NHTSA's regulations, which include the Federal Motor Vehicle Safety Standards to which new vehicles must be certified, do not generally prohibit or uniquely burden automated vehicles, with the possible exception of one rule regarding emergency flashers.

State vehicle codes probably do not prohibit—but may complicate—automated driving. These codes assume the presence of licensed human drivers who are able to exercise human judgment, and particular rules may functionally require that presence. New York somewhat uniquely directs a driver to keep one hand on the wheel at all times. In addition, far more common rules mandating reasonable, prudent, practicable, and safe driving have uncertain application to automated vehicles and their users. Following distance requirements may also restrict the lawful operation of tightly spaced vehicle platoons. Many of these issues arise even in the three states that expressly regulate automated vehicles.

The primary purpose of this paper is to assess the current legal status of automated vehicles. However, the paper includes draft language for US states that wish to clarify this status. It also recommends five near-term measures that may help increase legal certainty without producing premature regulation. First, regulators and standards organizations should develop common vocabularies and definitions that are useful in the legal, technical, and public realms. Second, the United States should closely monitor efforts to amend or interpret the 1969 Vienna Convention, which contains language similar to the Geneva Convention but does not bind the United States. Third, NHTSA should indicate the likely scope and schedule of potential regulatory action. Fourth, US states should analyze how their vehicle codes would or should apply to automated vehicles, including those that have an identifiable human operator and those that do not. Finally, additional research on laws applicable to trucks, buses, taxis, low-speed vehicles, and other specialty vehicles may be useful. This is in addition to ongoing research into the other legal aspects of vehicle automation.

2 Introduction

Imagine that someone invents a time machine. Does she break the law by using that machine to travel to the past? Whether the new technology is time machines or automated vehicles, the answer is not an automatic yes or no. Instead, that answer requires thoughtful consideration of existing law—and begins with the common law's presumption of legality. "There is no principle more essential to liberty, or more deeply imbued in our law, than that what is not prohibited, is permitted."[1] This fundamental principle finds its strongest application in criminal law: Courts strictly construe criminal statutes in part because there can be "no crime without law": "nullum crimen sine lege."[2] This principle is also recognized in other jurisdictions[3]—although perhaps less so in Germany.[4]

Until legislators, regulators, or judges definitively clarify the legal status of automated vehicles, any answer is necessarily a guess. But some guesses are more helpful than others, and unsupported assertions of illegality are particularly unhelpful.[5] These assertions substitute assumption for analysis and a presumption of illegality for the presumption of legality. Reaching a useful conclusion about the legal status of automated vehicles instead requires identification and interpretation of all laws that might conceivably prohibit (or be construed to prohibit) their manufacture, sale, or use. This paper attempts such an analysis, so while it begins with the presumption of legality, it seeks to prove a hypothesis of legality by disproving illegality.

Illegality in this sense refers to the proscription of conduct rather than to the mere assignment of responsibility for the costs of that conduct. This paper does not consider how the rules of tort could or should apply to automated vehicles—that is, the extent to which tort liability might shift upstream to companies responsible for the design, manufacture, sale, operation, or provision of data or other services to an automated vehicle.[6] Nonetheless, the legality of automated vehicles is foundational to these matters, because violation of certain laws under certain conditions can be used to establish negligence or defect[7] and, to a lesser extent, compliance with certain laws might limit liability.[8] Contract law, to which similar considerations may apply, is also outside this paper's scope.

The identification of relevant law is a rather large undertaking. Domestic law includes, at a minimum, the US constitution; federal statutes and certain treaties; regulations and practices of federal administrative agencies; constitutions of states, Native American tribes, and territories; statutes of these and other jurisdictions; regulations and practices of administrative agencies within these jurisdictions; and ordinances and other enactments of municipalities and other local authorities; as well as common law (i.e., case law) adopted and adapted by courts within all these jurisdictions.[9] International law is a separate system derived from (again at a minimum) treaties, custom, and general principles.[10]

This paper identifies three key legal regimes: the 1949 Geneva Convention on Road Traffic, regulations enacted by the National Highway Traffic Safety Administration, and the vehicle codes of US states (in tandem with model language supplied by the Uniform Vehicle Code[11]). It considers how these regimes might apply to both the sale of automated passenger cars and the operation of such vehicles on public roads in the United States. Its scope includes vehicle platoons,[12] which are discussed in an appendix,[13] but excludes trucks, buses, and taxicabs as well as all vehicles not operated on public roads.

Interpreting these laws is, in many ways, more challenging than merely identifying them. In domestic law, a statute is generally interpreted to carry out the will of the legislature that enacted it:

In all cases the object is to see what is the intention expressed by the words used. But, from the imperfection of language, it is impossible to know what that intention is without inquiring further, and seeing what the circumstances were with reference to which the words were used, and what was the object, appearing from those circumstances, which the person using them had in view; for the meaning of the word varies according to the circumstances with respect to which they were used.[14]

Courts avail themselves of numerous interpretive theories, techniques, and canons to arrive at results that are not necessarily obvious from the words of the statute itself.[15] For example, California's vehicle code provides that "[n]o person shall drive a vehicle upon a highway at" an unreasonably high speed[16] and expressly states that a bicycle is not a "vehicle."[17] Nonetheless, a California court held that a bicyclist could be convicted of speeding.[18] This is because the code also provides that "[e]very person riding a bicycle upon a highway has all the rights and is subject to all the provisions applicable to the driver of a vehicle [under the rules of the road] ... except those provisions which by their very nature can have no application."[19] The court concluded that "the clear legislative intent ... was to make bicycles subject to the same rules of the road as motor vehicles" and that "[t]o rule otherwise would inevitably frustrate the manifest purposes of the legislation as a whole and lead to absurd results."[20]

In international law, "[a] treaty shall be interpreted in good faith in accordance with the ordinary meaning to be given to the terms of the treaty in their context and in the light of its object and purpose."[21] That context includes, inter alia, the treaty's "text, including its preamble and annexes."[22] Together with that context, "[t]here shall be taken into account," inter alia, "any subsequent practice in the application of the treaty which establishes the agreement of the parties regarding its interpretation." In general, "[w]hen a treaty has been authenticated in two or more languages, the text is equally authoritative in each language."[23] Furthermore, "supplementary means of interpretation, including the preparatory work of the treaty," may be used to "confirm" a meaning "or to determine the meaning when the interpretation" would otherwise be "ambiguous or obscure" or produce "a result which is manifestly absurd or unreasonable."[24] For example, the European Court of Human Rights relied on history and context to interpret the term "alcoholics" as encompassing persons who might not be addicted to alcohol but "whose conduct and behavior under the influence of alcohol pose a threat to public order or themselves."[25] Since definitions matter, this paper turns to them now.

3   Automated Driving Requires No Real-Time Human Input

For the purpose of this paper, automated driving and automated operation each mean computer direction of a vehicle's steering, braking, and accelerating without real-time human input. An automated vehicle is a motor vehicle capable of automated driving.[26] As the remaining sections of this paper conclude, existing law does not categorically prohibit the sale or automated operation of such vehicles.

That conclusion is only one part of the paper's analysis. That is because the lack of real-time human input does not necessarily negate a human role in the vehicle's operation. Only in the narrowest transitive sense does driving refer exclusively to the direct physical manipulation of a motor vehicle's steering wheel, throttle, brake, clutch, and related mechanisms; one hopes that routine statements like "we drove to the beach" do not imply that these responsibilities are being shared at any given moment.

A more useful conception of driving recognizes all of its constituent elements. Primary tasks involve the selection of destinations and their order (trip), roads to those destinations (route), lanes as well as the turns and merges onto them (path), and speed and spacing within those lanes (position).[27] Secondary tasks involve the adjustment of safety features such as windshield wipers, lights, and turn signals.[28] Tertiary tasks involve the adjustment of comfort features such as the radio or air conditioning.[29] Vehicle propulsion—whether combustion or current—arguably adds a fourth set of driving tasks. Each of these tasks requires the perception of information, a decision based on that information, and the execution of that decision.[30]

In this way, a human-machine system may actually "drive" an automated vehicle: Some of the constituent tasks may be performed by a human, others by a machine, and still others by a combination—either sequential or simultaneous—of humans and machines.[31] This performance may occur in advance or in real time, remotely or in the vehicle, and independent of or in cooperation with other actors.[32] And it may vary depending on the particular domain of operation.[33]

Properly conceptualizing this system has been a key first step in a number of efforts, including a particularly relevant German project.[34] Some groups have attempted to draw a single bright line between conventional and automated vehicles.[35] Some have defined multiple levels of automation.[36] Some have recognized multiple dimensions.[37] Others have yet to determine their approach.[38] And at least one rejects the enterprise altogether.[39] Even the terminology used is contentious.[40]

Regardless of how it is described, the idea of a human-machine system is critical to the paper's full analysis. This analysis assumes that such a system is technically capable of driving in a manner that would be considered reasonable today.[41] To this end, the particular division of tasks between human and machine is a technical question: A human must perform those tasks that the machine cannot. But it is also a legal question: A human may be required to perform certain tasks regardless of what the machine can do or is doing. These two questions are distinct.[42]

This paper asks whether the division of tasks that is legally required deviates from the division of tasks that is technically required. In other words, does existing law impose obligations on the human user of an automated vehicle that are not technically necessary? For example, an automated vehicle may be technically able to operate without a human present, but that operation might only be legal if a licensed human driver is in the driver's seat.[43]

Four levels of human participation in driving help simplify this analysis. In the first, no human is available to provide real-time input to the automated vehicle—perhaps because she is asleep or at home. In the second, a human is physically present and able to provide such input whenever she desires. In the third, that human is monitoring the vehicle and is available to provide such input at some point after the vehicle requests it. And in the fourth, that human is monitoring the vehicle's environment and is available to provide real-time input immediately, regardless of whether the vehicle requests it. These levels can variously describe what a human is actually doing, what she is technically required to be doing, and what she is legally required (or legally presumed) to be doing.

As a general matter, the automation, delegation, or division of work previously performed by a single person is hardly new to law. The most instructive model for automation may actually be corporatization—that is, how law has addressed notions of specialization, control, and responsibility among multiple human and nonhuman actors in complex systems.[44] Particularly relevant examples may include corporate personhood, the identity of an investor under patent law, and, potentially, regulation of high-speed electronic trading.[45] This paper begins its legal analysis with a treaty directed at an earlier instance of automation, namely the automobile.

4 The Convention on Road Traffic Does Not Categorically Prohibit Automated Driving

The 1949 Geneva Convention on Road Traffic, to which the United States is a party, promotes road safety by establishing uniform rules. These rules include article 8, which requires every vehicle or combination thereof to have a driver who is "at all times ... able to control" it.[46] The 1968 Vienna Convention on Road Traffic, to which the United States is not a party, contains similar language that might be clarified by amendment.[47] Article 8 of the Geneva Convention is probably satisfied if a human is able to intervene in operation of the vehicle and possibly satisfied if that vehicle operates within the bounds of human judgment.[48] However, because the Convention is binding internationally and may be binding domestically, clarification of these issues is desirable.[49]

4.1 The Geneva Convention's History Informs Article 8's Driver Rule

The Convention on Road Traffic signed at Geneva in 1949,[50] best known in connection with one type of international driving permit,[51] was intended to "promot[e] the development and safety of international road traffic by establishing certain uniform rules."[52] The "[r]ules of the road" contained in chapter II of the treaty are directed at domestic as well as international traffic; they constitute "minimum regulations which would be observed by vehicles traveling inside the borders of their country of origin so that foreign motorists would know roughly what standard of behavior to expect."[53] Most of these rules are directed at "the driver."[54] The provisions of particular interest are contained in article 8, which reads as follows:

> 1. *Every vehicle or combination of vehicles proceeding as a unit shall have a driver.*

2. Draught, pack or saddle animals shall have a driver, and cattle shall be accompanied, except in special areas which shall be marked at the points of entry.
3. Convoys of vehicles and animals shall have the number of drivers prescribed by domestic regulations.
4. Convoys shall, if necessary, be divided into sections of moderate length, and be sufficiently spaced out for the convenience of traffic. This provision does not apply to regions where migration of nomads occurs.
5. *Drivers shall at all times be able to control their vehicles* or guide their animals. When approaching other road users, they shall take such precautions as may be required for the safety of the latter.[55]

Article 4 defines driver as "any person who drives a vehicle, including cycles, or guides draught, pack or saddle animals or herds or flocks on a road, or who is in actual physical control of the same."[56] Motor vehicle is also defined; vehicle is not.[57]

The origin of these provisions is illuminating. The 1949 treaty was drafted under the auspices of the Economic and Social Council of the United Nations to "terminate and replace, in relations between the Contracting States, the International Convention relative to Motor Traffic and the International Convention relative to Road Traffic signed at Paris on 24 April 1926, and the Convention of Inter-American Automotive Traffic opened for signature at Washington on 15 December 1943."[58] The 1926 Motor Traffic Convention, for its part, modified the Convention with Respect to the International Circulation of Motor Vehicles signed at Paris in 1909.[59] (Of these earlier treaties, the Inter-American Convention[60] is the only one to which the United States is a party.[61]) The negotiators at Geneva proceeded from a draft treaty that had been prepared within the Economic Commission for Europe.[62] The ECE drafters "kept constantly in mind and were guided by the ideas contained in" the 1943 Convention[63] but were clearly influenced by the Paris treaties as well.[64]

Without recorded discussion, the Geneva committee responsible for what would become article 8 adopted the ECE draft's requirements that "[e]very vehicle or combination of vehicles proceeding as a unit ... have a driver" and that "[d]rivers ... at all times be able ... to control their vehicles or guide their animals."[65] These draft provisions come from two articles in the 1926 Road Traffic Convention (which are themselves based on a French draft prepared for the conference that produced both 1926 treaties).[66] Article 2 provides in part that "[e]very vehicle proceeding singly must have a driver," and article 3 provides in part that "[d]rivers shall at all times be able and in a position to control their vehicle or guide their teams or draught, pack or saddle animals." Significantly, these express requirements are absent from the three treaties that address only motor vehicles.[67]

This history suggests that article 8 was addressed to unsupervised animals (including animal-powered vehicles) rather than to unsupervised automobiles. As a practical matter, cows, sheep, mules, and horses (with or without carts in tow) might be perfectly capable of reaching their destination without human control.[68] Cars were not. Even the visionary behind the General Motors Futurama at the 1939-40 World's Exhibition stopped short of predicting a truly driverless car:

> [T]hese cars of 1960 and the highways on which they drive will have in them devices which will correct the faults of human beings as drivers. They will prevent the driver from committing errors. They will prevent his turning out into traffic except when he should. They will aid him in passing through intersections without

slowing down or causing anyone else to do so and without endangering himself or others.[69]

In 1949 (as in 1926), deliberately requiring a motor vehicle to have a driver would have seemed as important as deliberately requiring that vehicle to maintain contact with the ground. Indeed, all of these rules "were of such a general nature and were so widely accepted that it was not considered any difficulty would result in having them applicable to all traffic."[70]

Obviousness may also explain why the Geneva negotiators spent little time discussing the definition of "driver" in article 4. The 1909 and 1926 treaties do not expressly define this (or any other) term. In the 1943 Inter-American Convention, "operator" means "any person who drives or is in actual physical control of a motor vehicle upon a highway."[71] This phrase probably came from the Uniform Vehicle Code developed in the United States earlier in the century.[72] The ECE draft drew on this language to define "driver" as "any person who drives a vehicle, including cycles, or guides draught, pack or saddle animals or herds or flocks on the road, or who is in actual physical control of the same."[73] After negotiators "observed that no Committee had considered" this definition, the French representative on the committee that was subsequently assigned this task pointed out "that to define driver ... as a person who drove, was not to define the word at all."[74] Her fellow representatives helpfully responded by adopting the draft language and "leaving to the Special Group the question of the modification of the wording of the French text to meet the objection raised by the French representative."[75] Accordingly, the English definition remains somewhat circular, while in the equally authoritative French text "conducteur" means "toutes personnes qui *assument la direction de véhicules* ... ou qui en ont la maîtrise effective."[76]

4.2   The Vienna Convention May Also Inform Interpretation of This Rule

Of the 95 states that are currently parties to the Geneva Convention,[77] 40 are also parties to the Convention on Road Traffic signed at Vienna in 1968.[78] The United States is neither a party nor a signatory to and hence has no obligations under this 1968 treaty. Nonetheless, this Vienna Convention may be useful to the extent that it reveals the practice of the Geneva Convention parties with respect to that treaty.[79] In this regard, it is important to note that the United States remains a member of the United Nations Economic Commission for Europe (UNECE), under the auspices of which at least the Vienna Convention continues to be discussed and amended.[80]

In comparison to the Geneva Convention, the Vienna Convention imposes somewhat more extensive obligations on the driver of a vehicle. Article 8 reads as follows:

> 1. Every moving vehicle or combination of vehicles shall have a driver.
>
> 2. It is recommended that domestic legislation should provide that pack, draught or saddle animals, and, except in such special areas as may be marked at the entry, cattle, singly or in herds, or flocks, shall have a driver.
>
> 3. Every driver shall possess the necessary physical and mental ability and be in a fit physical and mental condition to drive.
>
> 4. Every driver of a power-driven vehicle shall possess the knowledge and skill necessary for driving the vehicle; however, this requirement shall not be a bar to driving practice by learner-drivers in conformity with domestic legislation.

> 5. Every driver shall at all times be able to control his vehicle or to guide his animals.[81]

A sixth paragraph on distracted driving was added to this article in 2006:

> A driver of a vehicle shall at all times minimize any activity other than driving. Domestic legislation should lay down rules on the use of phones by drivers of vehicles. In any case, legislation shall prohibit the use by a driver of a motor vehicle or moped of a hand-held phone while the vehicle is in motion.[82]

In addition, article 13 provides in part that "[e]very driver of a vehicle shall in all circumstances have his vehicle under control so as to be able to exercise due and proper care and to be at all times in a position to perform all manoeuvres required of him."[83]

Article 1 defines driver as "any person who drives a motor vehicle or other vehicle (including a cycle), or who guides cattle, singly or in herds, or flocks, or draught, pack or saddle animals on a road."[84] This definition omits the American-inspired reference to "actual physical control" found in the Geneva Convention.[85] As with the Geneva Convention, motor vehicle is also defined; vehicle is not.[86]

Through the UNECE, parties to the Vienna Convention have been debating its application to driver assistance systems for at least a decade.[87] The "German position" in 2002 was that only systems that can be overridden by the driver at any time are permitted under that treaty.[88] According to a report prepared for the German project group described above,[89] this view of the Vienna Convention would only permit a driver assistance system that is continuously monitored by a driver who is aware of the current traffic situation at all times and who has the actual ability to override that system.[90]

Under a contrary view, the Vienna Convention does not necessarily prohibit every system that a driver cannot override.[91] This is because, first, the Vienna Convention's "rules of the road" are "merely obligations of conduct for the driver that are not applicable to" the actual design of a motor vehicle and, second, the authentic treaty language (including "control" in the English and "contrôler/maîtriser" in the French)[92] is more broadly suggestive of monitoring and supervision than the common German translation ("Beherrschen").[93] Switzerland and the Netherlands have argued that even a system that determines the vehicle's speed and position would not contravene the treaty, because the driver would still maintain full control of the vehicle itself.[94]

The Vienna Convention might be amended again to provide clarity regarding driver assistance systems. For example, a 2011 proposal by an informal expert group would have defined "[d]riving assistance system" as "a built-in system intended to help the driver in performing his driving task and which have an influence on the way the vehicle is driven, especially aimed at the prevention of road accidents" and specified that such systems "shall not be considered contrary to" articles 8 and 13 as long as they "are overridable at any time or can be switched off," only optimize a function performed by the driver, operate only in case of emergency, or intervene in a way that is "identical with a usual property of a motor vehicle (e.g. speed limiting device)."[95]

Although this proposal was apparently "delete[d]," it has remained the subject of discussion into 2012.[96] It is important to note that a state that is party to both the Geneva and Vienna Conventions would not directly alter its obligations under the former treaty by accepting an amendment of the latter.

4.3   The Term "Driver" Is Probably Flexible

The identity of an automated vehicle's driver is probably a more important question under US state law than under the Geneva Convention. This is a curious assertion, since of these regimes only the Geneva Convention expressly requires vehicles to have drivers. But as the later discussion of domestic law demonstrates,[97] the devil is in the details, and when it came to the rules of the road, the Geneva negotiators deliberately avoided both devils and details.[98] By codifying basic expectations rather than precise mechanics, they achieved a consensus that has avoided amendment for more than sixty years.

This focus on fundamentals is consistent with a broad and flexible understanding of the term "driver" as defined in article 4 and used throughout the treaty. Like many of the US state definitions that probably share a common ancestor,[99] article 4's definition contemplates both "driv[ing]" and "actual physical control."[100] And it is nonexclusive, referring to "any" person rather than to "the" person.[101] An automated vehicle might therefore have multiple simultaneous drivers, including a person who is physically or electronically positioned to provide real-time input to the vehicle, a person who turns on or dispatches the vehicle, or a person who initiates or customizes that automated operation.[102]

As a definitional matter, these persons might even be nonhuman. International law recognizes corporate persons in the context of investor protection[103] and human rights (including the 1950 European Convention for the Protection of Human Rights and Fundamental Freedoms).[104] In this way, the companies responsible for the design, manufacture, or ongoing operation of an automated vehicle may constitute drivers for the purpose of the Geneva Convention.[105] In contrast, the treatment of a computer system as a driver seems much more speculative in light of article 4's reference to a "person,"[106] and indeed Germany has expressly rejected such an approach to the Vienna Convention.[107]

The drafters of the Geneva Convention did presume that drivers would be physically proximate to their vehicles or animals; the treaty describes drivers intransitively "keep[ing]" or "mov[ing]" to the edge of the carriageway,[108] "turn[ing] into a road,"[109] and "approaching other road users,"[110] and it requires every motor vehicle to "be so constructed that the driver shall be able to see ahead, to the right and to the left, clearly enough to enable him to drive safely,"[111] with "at least one mirror ... so placed as to enable [him] to view from his seat the road to the rear of the vehicle."[112] But these rules do not necessarily define the whole set of drivers under the treaty—or even the whole set of lawful drivers.[113]

Ultimately, the dual questions of who a driver is and what she must do are intertwined with each other and woven into the larger fabric of the Geneva Convention. The concept of control informs this task—and is the focus of the section that follows.

4.4   Article 8 Can Faithfully Be Interpreted to Require Only Indirect Control

The obligations imposed by the Geneva Convention are intended to foster road safety in part by ensuring that vehicles can be controlled.[114] Control in this sense is a relative concept.[115] This suggests that article 8 is probably satisfied if a human is able to intervene in operation of the vehicle[116] and possibly satisfied if that vehicle operates within the bounds of human judgment.[117] These interpretations may not require a human to be physically present.[118]

4.4.1   The Purpose of Control Is to Facilitate Safety

With respect to article 8, the interpretive task is clear even if the answer is not: In the light of the Geneva Convention's "object and purpose"[119] of "promoting the development and safety of international road traffic by establishing certain uniform rules,"[120] what contextual "ordinary meaning"[121] should be given to the requirement that "[e]very vehicle or combination of vehicles proceeding as a unit shall have a driver" who is "at all times ... able to control" her vehicle or combination of vehicles[122]—or, in the equally authoritative French, "[t]out véhicule ou ensemble de véhicules couplés marchant isolément doit avoir un conducteur," qui "doive[] constamment avoir le contrôle de [sa] véhicule ou pouvoir guider [ses] animaux"?[123]

It is apparent that the Geneva Convention is to be interpreted in a way that promotes rather than frustrates road safety. This conclusion is manifest from the treaty's preamble, from its preparatory work, and from the context provided by the entirety of article 8's fifth paragraph: "Drivers shall at all times be able to control their vehicles or guide their animals. When approaching other road users, they shall take such precautions as may be required for the safety of the latter."[124] If automated vehicles ultimately deliver a safety breakthrough, an interpretation of article 8 that prohibits their use would produce "a result which is manifestly absurd or unreasonable."[125] Indeed, such technologies may well constitute "precautions ... required for the safety of" other road users.[126]

As its fifth paragraph makes clear, article 8 promotes safety through control. To control is "[t]o exercise restraint or direction upon the free action of; to hold sway over, exercise power or authority over; to dominate, command."[127] As one US court has noted, "[t]he essence of 'control' is nothing less than the power to determine the scope, range, or effect of a given activity."[128]

With respect to road traffic in general and animals in particular,[129] control would seem to serve two purposes. First, it facilitates compliance with the written rules of the road: Unlike a horse, a human can be expected to keep a vehicle on the proper side of the road (and to know whether that side is the left or the right).[130] Second, it facilitates reasonable judgment in situations not expressly contemplated by those rules: Unlike a horse, a human can be expected to always "slow down or stop whenever circumstances so require, and particularly when visibility is not good."[131]

Control in this sense is a function rather than a device or mechanism.[132] Article 4 defines a driver as "any person who drives a vehicle, including cycles, or guides draught, pack or saddle animals or herds or flocks on a road, or who is in actual physical control of the same."[133] This language implies, first, that there is a difference between control and "actual physical control" and, second, that a person can be a driver without having "actual physical control" of her vehicle.[134] Indeed, "drive" means both "[t]o guide a vehicle or the animal that draws it" and "to travel or be conveyed in a carriage under one's own direction or at one's disposal."[135]

The French text leads to a similar conclusion by a slightly different route. Article 8 requires the driver to have "contrôle," which suggests supervision, monitoring, or mastery,[136] rather than "direction," which instead implies "complete power."[137] In contrast, article 4 specifies that "direction" and "maîtrise effective" are each sufficient but not necessary for a person to be a driver.[138]

State practice recognizes that control need not be direct or absolute. In addition to horses, antilock brakes[139] and electronic stability control[140] each mediate between a driver and her vehicle. Both the United States and the European Union (among others) require these nonequestrian technologies on certain vehicles.[141] In one sense, these systems actually reduce a driver's control over components of her vehicle. In another sense, they increase her control over the path and position of that vehicle. Control—like automation[142]—is a complex spectrum.

4.4.2 Control Is Generally Regarded as Relative

The requisite degree of control has arisen in other legal contexts. The vehicle codes of US states, which are discussed below, are particularly relevant.[143] In the time between the 1926 and 1949 treaties, Congress also passed two acts related to securities that also referenced "control" without defining it. Legislative history suggests that this omission was deliberate:

> [W]hen reference is made to "control," the term is intended to include actual control as well as what has been called legally enforceable control.... It was thought undesirable to attempt to define the term. It would be difficult if not impossible to enumerate or to anticipate the many ways in which actual control may be exerted. A few examples of the methods used are stock ownership, lease, contract, and agency. It is well known that actual control sometimes may be exerted through ownership of much less than a majority of the stock of a corporation either by the ownership of such stock alone or through such ownership in combination with other factors.[144]

The US Securities and Exchange Commission (SEC) ultimately defined "control" in a related context as "the possession, direct or indirect, of the power to direct or cause the direction of the management and policies of a person, whether through the ownership of voting securities, by contract, or otherwise."[145]

In international law, the International Court of Justice (ICJ), the International Tribunal for the Former Yugoslavia (ITFY)'s Appeals Chamber, the Iran-United States Claim Tribunal, and the European Court of Human Rights have all addressed the "problem of the degree of State control necessary for the purposes of attribution of conduct to the State."[146] "With regard to individuals or groups not organised into military structures," courts generally "have not considered an overall or general level of control to be sufficient, but have instead insisted upon specific instructions or directives aimed at the commission of specific acts, or have required public approval of those acts following their commission."[147]

However, the ICJ and the ITFY have disagreed vigorously about whether this "effective control" test also applies to military and paramilitary groups. The ICJ concluded that it does.[148] In contrast, the ITFY, emphasizing that the requisite "degree of control may ... vary according to the factual circumstances of each case,"[149] determined that an "overall control" test could be satisfied by "prov[ing] that the State wields overall control over the group, not only by equipping and financing the group, but also by coordinating or helping in the general planning of its military activity" even if the state did not "issue ... instructions for the commission of specific acts contrary to international law."[150]

4.4.3   Article 8 Requires at Most the Ability to Intervene

The judicial disagreement just discussed introduces the challenge of drawing lines in a way that faithfully interprets article 8: With how much specificity and concurrency must drivers "at all times be able to control their vehicles"?

Three key conclusions about the nature of control seem appropriate. First, control is more than a legal fiction: The mere designation of a driver for the purpose of legal responsibility—the approach adopted by Nevada, Florida, and California[151]—might fail to satisfy article 8's fifth paragraph even if it satisfied the first.

Second, being "able to control" does not mean actively exercising that control: To assert "that control may not, by definition, include the concept of fixing within its ambit is a bit like saying the volume control on a radio only 'controls' the volume if it is constantly increasing or decreasing the volume."[152] Operation of a vehicle without the driver's constant supervision would not necessarily violate article 8.

Third, control is limited by the characteristics of that which is being controlled: A carriage driver is not unable to control her vehicle simply because she cannot make her horse move as fast as the motor vehicles passing her. Similarly, a truck driver is not unable to control her truck simply because she cannot stop it as quickly or turn it as sharply as she could a car. Operation of a vehicle subject to certain limitations on the method, scope, or effect of the driver's input would not necessarily violate article 8.[153]

In short, article 8 could be faithfully interpreted to permit the operation of a vehicle that determines its own path and position in the presence of a person who is technically able to override those determinations. Conversely, an interpretation of article 8 that prohibits the operation of such a vehicle could be unreasonable if that interpretation ultimately frustrates road safety.

4.4.4   Operation Within the Bounds of Human Judgment May Also Suffice

Article 8 may also be susceptible to a more permissive interpretation, namely that any vehicle operating within the bounds of human judgment is being driven and controlled in a general sense, regardless of whether a person is present for or attentive to that operation. This interpretation treats automation as an enhancement of vehicle control rather than as an abdication of that control. Key to this conception is the same desire for safety through standardization that led the parties to the Geneva Convention to "establish[] certain uniform rules."[154]

Rather than negate decisions about a vehicle's path and position, automation changes how—and possibly when and by whom—those decisions are made. Electronic stability control and antilock brakes increase control by making the vehicle do what the driver wants rather than what she says.[155] Higher levels of automation would extend this approach. Under ideal road and traffic conditions, automated vehicles might facilitate uniform compliance with concrete rules of the road: In theory, they would stop at stop signs and yield to pedestrians. And under conditions that are less than ideal, they might facilitate decisions that are more deliberate, proactive, and consistent than those reached spontaneously by humans: Again in theory, they would take the kind of precautions for which they are programmed. These parameters would control such a vehicle's behavior, and a person who directs that vehicle to drive itself (i.e., the driver) would be effectively instructing it to operate under that control.

This interpretation depends on unproven assumptions about nascent technologies. Ultimately, however, this field may develop to the point where the certification of technology to implement standard rules of the road is not conceptually different from—and in fact empirically preferable to—the licensing of drivers to implement those same rules. The same could not be said of the horses, mules, sheep, cows, and geese that were unlikely to listen to whatever rules the drafters of the 1926 Road Traffic Convention saw fit to prescribe.[156]

4.5   Article 8 May Nonetheless Arise Internationally or Domestically

The previous part concluded that article 8 probably does not prohibit automated vehicles. However, if this conclusion is incorrect—or if certain actors believe it to be either incorrect or insufficiently manifest—questions about the Convention may nonetheless arise internationally or domestically. Article 8 is mandatory rather than merely hortatory,[157] it is clearly binding as international law,[158] and it is probably binding as federal law.[159] Regardless, US actors could conceivably influence the treaty's interpretation or clarify its domestic application.[160]

4.5.1   Article 8 Is Mandatory

The legal status of chapter II's rules of the road (which include article 8) received considerable attention at the Geneva conference—though perhaps not as much as that given to cycles, lights, and lights on cycles.[161] Negotiators struggled with, and at times seem to have conflated, several questions:

1. Were these rules intended to apply to domestic traffic?

2. Would each state be internationally obligated to harmonize its domestic law with these rules?

3. Would a state commit an internationally wrongful act every time a driver within its territory violated any of these rules?

4. What status would these rules themselves have within each state's domestic law?

The answers are, now, surprisingly straightforward:

1. Yes.

2. Yes.

3. No.

4. It depends—but as a matter of international law, it simply doesn't matter.

Much of the discussion regarding chapter II's rules of the road was in connection with the treaty's premier article, which was ultimately formulated as follows:

> 1. While reserving its jurisdiction over the use of
> its own roads, each Contracting State agrees to

the use of its roads for international traffic under the conditions set out in this Convention.

2. No Contracting State shall be required to extend the benefit of the provisions of this Convention to any motor vehicle or trailer, or to any driver having remained within its territory for a continuous period exceeding one year.[162]

The United States initially took the position that "the Convention applied to international, and not to internal, traffic."[163] Indeed, "[i]t was on that basis, and that basis alone, that the United States Government was participating in the Conference," because "internal traffic was regulated by the [varying] legislation of the forty-eight states."[164] Nonetheless, the United States ultimately accepted that "the purpose of chapter II was to establish, in effect, an international code of minimum safety requirements. By indirection, the rules of the road set forth in the convention would apply to the pattern of domestic as well as to international traffic."[165]

The general opinion at the conference was that these rules would be mandatory, "for if they were not legally binding they could be of no practical value."[166] To wit:

> Mr. FAIRBANK (United States of America) said that if the Convention was adopted and ratified by his country, it would become the law of the land both for its own inhabitants and for visitors, and each State would endeavour to enforce it to the best of its ability. Undoubtedly, as the Convention was general in scope, it could not cover every possible situation, and his country would, if necessary, enact more detailed laws, either Federal or State, for application whenever required.[167]

Although individual drivers (for the most part) are the intended subjects of these substantive rules, states are the primary subjects of international law. The United Kingdom therefore expressed concern that a state would commit an internationally wrongful act every time a driver within its territory violated any of chapter II's rules of the road:

> Governments could enact legislation in order to comply with [these rules], but they could not ensure that such laws would not be violated. Nor, to take another example, could governments ensure that "Drivers shall, at all times, be able and in a position to control their vehicles or guide their animals".... No government, however totalitarian, could ensure that a driver was always in full control of his vehicle.[168]

Article 6, which provides that each party "shall take appropriate measures to ensure the observance of the rules set out in" chapter II, was a direct response to the United Kingdom's concern.[169] As discussed below, this is an important point: Article 6 was added to clarify that each individual rule violation is not necessarily a treaty violation;[170] it was not added to specify a particular means by which each state would give effect to those obligations within its domestic law. The latter is simply not an ordinary question of international law.[171]

4.5.2   The Convention Is Binding as International Law

"Every treaty in force is binding upon the parties to it and must be performed by them in good faith."[172] As one of 95 states to ratify the Geneva Convention, the United States is obligated under international law to "take appropriate measures to ensure the observance"[173] within its territory of the rule that "[e]very vehicle or combination of vehicles proceeding as a unit ... have a driver" and that "[d]rivers ... at all times be able to control their vehicles or guide their animals."[174] By violating this obligation in the absence of circumstances precluding wrongfulness,[175] the United States would be committing an internationally wrongful act for which it would be internationally responsible.[176] That responsibility, in turn, would entail a secondary obligation to cease and make reparations for the wrongful act.[177]

In a battle between the technology and the treaty, the technology seems the likely winner, though this prediction is admittedly more consistent with developments in the United States than with developments in Europe.[178] Regardless, this part briefly considers, in rough order of their likelihood, six ways that states might clarify the content or curtail the application of the Geneva Convention. Four are ordinary, two are remote, and none is exclusive of another.

First, governments might tend individually to facilitate or simply tolerate the use of automated vehicles on public roadways, either with or without expressly concluding that such use is consistent with the treaty. Widespread state practice of this sort could indicate that the proper interpretation of the treaty is one that prohibits automated vehicles no more than antilock brakes, electronic stability control, drive-by-wire, and other systems that attenuate a driver's physical control of the vehicle. Conversely, governments might tend individually to cite the Geneva Convention in limiting the use of automated vehicles, which could suggest the correctness of a more restrictive interpretation.

Second, certain states might seek to collectively "clarify" the Convention. Although the treaty provides no formal mechanism for clarification (as opposed to amendment), a group of states might, in an effort to establish state practice, announce that the treaty, in their view, is either consistent or inconsistent with the use of automated vehicles.

Third, states might seek to formally amend the Convention so that it is clearly consistent with the use of automated vehicles. Under article 31, any state may propose an amendment; if two-thirds of the parties accept it (in the case that no conference is called), that amendment becomes binding among all parties that do not timely object.[179] Notably, since 40 states are parties to both the Geneva Convention and the Vienna Convention, efforts to amend one might complement efforts to amend the other.

Fourth, a state might simply withdraw from the Geneva Convention: Under article 32's denunciation procedure, a state need only give one year's notice.[180] This may be conceivable if the Vienna Convention is (again) amended but the Geneva Convention is not. The practical consequences of denunciation may be limited; currently, for example, it would not be obvious to a German driver visiting the United States or to a US driver visiting Germany that only one of these states is a party to the Geneva Convention.[181]

Fifth, the Economic and Social Council (ECOSOC), the UN organ through which the Geneva conference was conducted, might request an advisory opinion from the International Court of Justice (ICJ) on the meaning of the Geneva Convention's relevant provisions.[182] In its history, ECOSOC has requested two advisory opinions.[183] Given the ICJ's slow speed, however, cars might be flying before the court reached a final decision.

Sixth, an actual dispute might arise among parties to the Geneva Convention. Two scenarios are conceivable. In one, a party would argue that the United States violated (and continues to violate) its treaty obligations through the enactment (and continued existence) of domestic laws that expressly permit the operation of automated vehicles on public roads. These laws, though made by subnational governments, constitute action by the United States under international law.[184] In the other (potentially overlapping) scenario, a state would exercise diplomatic protection on behalf of a national[185] injured by an automated vehicle while in the United States.[186] In both scenarios, the state that believed itself aggrieved might protest, seek consultations, or ultimately apply to the ICJ for a decision pursuant to article 33 of the Geneva Convention.[187]

4.5.3   The Convention Is Probably Binding and Enforceable as Federal Law

The remainder of this part analyzes the Geneva Convention as federal rather than merely international law. It considers how article 8 might be domestically relevant,[188] and how courts might address questions of self-execution,[189] standing,[190] and constitutionality.[191] In contrast to the foregoing discussion, it generally uses the term "state" to refer to US states rather than to countries.

4.5.3.1   Article 8 May Be Considered by Domestic Actors

Article 8 could arise in several domestic contexts. Of the four scenarios introduced below, only the final one would require that the Geneva Convention be self-executing;[192] the first three, to varying and variable extents, arguably represent "softer" uses of this treaty in the domestic sphere.

First, government actors might simply exercise their respective authority in a way that complies with their understanding of the treaty. For example, the National Highway Traffic Safety Administration might require that all vehicles be manufactured with speed and steering controls that are useable by a human. Or a governor may veto a bill declaring that automated vehicles need not have a human driver in a technical or legal sense. There are many potential explanations for this subtle deference: That governor, for example, may believe that she is bound by international law,[193] that she is bound by federal law,[194] or that such comity is prudent or appropriate even if it is not mandatory.[195]

Second, a court applying statutory or regulatory law might interpret that law in a way that is consistent with its understanding of the Geneva Convention. For example, it might hold that even an automated vehicle has a human driver under a state's vehicle code. Or, it might use the language of article 8 to conclude that the state code implicitly requires human control of every vehicle.[196] This approach reflects the longstanding principle, expressed in *Murray v. The Charming Betsy*, that "an act of Congress ought never to be construed to violate the law of nations if any other possible construction remains."[197]

Third, a court might consider the Geneva Convention otherwise relevant to certain elements of a cause of action (or an affirmative defense thereto), particularly duty, breach, and causation. In at least three cases, courts have discussed the Convention in the course of rejecting a plaintiff's claim that a rental agency negligently entrusted a vehicle to a foreign driver.[198] In a fourth case, the court held that the defendant, a Mexican citizen who had "lived in the United States for two years" but had only a driver's license from Mexico, could not legally drive under the Geneva Convention.[199] And in a fifth case, an Illinois court held that the defendant, a Canadian citizen who obtained a Canadian driver's license after revocation of his Illinois license, had been properly convicted of "driving while his license was revoked."[200]

Finally, a court might be asked to decide whether the Geneva Convention precludes a federal agency, a state legislature, or a state agency from expressly permitting or actively facilitating the use of automated vehicles on public roads.[201] The court may face this question through an action under the federal Administrative Procedure Act (APA), under a state equivalent, or under the US constitution.

The federal APA governs actions taken by federal agencies, including the National Highway Traffic Safety Administration (NHTSA). 5 U.S.C. § 706 provides that:

> To the extent necessary to decision and when presented, the reviewing court shall decide all

relevant questions of law, interpret constitutional and statutory provisions, and determine the meaning or applicability of the terms of an agency action. The reviewing court shall ... hold unlawful and set aside agency action, findings, and conclusions found to be— (A) arbitrary, capricious, an abuse of discretion, or otherwise not in accordance with law; (B) contrary to constitutional right, power, privilege, or immunity; (C) in excess of statutory jurisdiction, authority, or limitations, or short of statutory right....[202]

At least one federal court has enforced a self-executing treaty through the APA,[203] and scholars have endorsed the viability of such a claim.[204]

Action by a state agency is typically subject to corresponding review under state law. The 2010 Revised Model State Administrative Procedure Act provides that a "court may grant relief only if it determines that" the state agency has prejudiced the plaintiff by "erroneously interpret[ing] the law" or by taking action that is "arbitrary, capricious, an abuse of discretion, or otherwise not in accordance with law," among other grounds.[205] A court applying Nevada law considers whether the agency's final decision is "[i]n violation of constitutional or statutory provisions," "[i]n excess of the statutory authority of the agency," or "affected by other error of law," among other grounds.[206] In California, "[e]ach regulation adopted, to be effective, shall be within the scope of authority conferred and in accordance with standards prescribed by other provisions of law."[207] And in Florida, "[a]ny person substantially affected by a rule or a proposed rule may seek an administrative determination of the invalidity of the rule on the ground that the rule is an invalid exercise of delegated legislative authority."[208]

State statutes as well as state regulations may be subject to challenge directly under the supremacy clause of the US constitution. This is an open question—and a confusing concept.[209] In general, a plaintiff must have authority to assert a legal theory about a matter over which the court has jurisdiction. In a challenge to a final rule adopted by a federal agency, for example, 5 U.S.C. § 702[210] might provide that authority, 5 U.S.C. § 706[211] might provide, at least in part, that legal theory, and 28 U.S.C. § 1331[212] might provide that jurisdiction. However, not every injured person is entitled to assert every legal theory; only a government, for example, can criminally prosecute a burglar.[213] Now consider a challenge to a state statute expressly permitting driverless vehicles: What authorizes a private party to argue that the Geneva Convention trumps that statute under the supremacy clause? The answer may be that this authority is implicit in the legal theory itself—that is, the Convention or the supremacy clause evinces what is known as an implied cause of action.[214]

One possibility is that the Geneva Convention's incorporation into federal law implies this authority.[215] This question is, or at least should be, distinct from the question of whether the Convention is self-executing—that is, whether it can supply a legal theory.[216] Indeed, in prior cases, the Convention generally arises as a defense rather than as a basis for the action.[217] Nonetheless, in light of judicial aversion both to vindicating treaties within domestic law[218] and to finding implied statutory causes of action,[219] this possibility appears remote.

The other possibility is that the supremacy clause of the US constitution implies this authority. The US Supreme Court recently declined to decide this question, returning it to the Court of Appeals for the Ninth Circuit. In *Douglas v. Independent Living Center of Southern California*, certain Medicaid providers and beneficiaries argued that statutory changes to California's Medicaid plan violate a federal statutory condition under which Congress funds this joint state-federal program. The Ninth Circuit held that the plaintiffs could bring an action directly under the supremacy clause (rather than under a statutory cause of action).[220] After the Supreme Court granted certiorari to review that particular holding, the federal agency responsible for reviewing state Medicaid plans approved some of California's changes. Citing this approval, a narrow majority[221] of the Supreme Court then vacated the Ninth Circuit judgments and remanded the cases for argument on whether "these cases may proceed directly under the Supremacy Clause now that the agency has acted."[222] The four dissenters[223] objected that agency action was irrelevant to the question on which the court had granted certiorari, and they argued that the answer to this question should be that "[w]hen Congress did not intend to provide a private right of action to enforce a statute enacted under the Spending Clause, the Supremacy Clause does not supply one of its own force."[224]

Raising the Geneva Convention in court might in turn raise three related issues, which are discussed in the three sections that follow.

4.5.3.2   *The Convention Is Probably Self-Executing*

As part 4.5.2 noted, ratification of the Geneva Convention was an international act by which the United States committed itself to assuming certain international obligations.[225] But ratification was also a domestic act by which the president, "by and with the advice and consent of the Senate,"[226] made the Geneva Convention part of federal law. The so-called "supremacy clause" of the US constitution declares that:

> This Constitution, and the Laws of the United States which shall be made in pursuance thereof; and all treaties made, or which shall be made, under the authority of the United States, shall be the supreme law of the land; and the judges in every state shall be bound thereby,

anything in the constitution or laws of any state
to the contrary notwithstanding.[227]

Notwithstanding this supremacy clause, the Supreme Court
has divided international agreements into two domestic
categories: "self-executing treaties (those 'equivalent to an act
of the legislature') and non-self-executing treaties (those 'the
legislature must execute' to have domestic effect)."[228]
According to the court in *Medellin v. Texas*, a treaty is either
self-executing or non-self-executing in its entirety (a
conclusion that appears to depart from earlier case law),[229]
and only self-executing treaties can be applied by domestic
courts as US law.[230] Absent strong indications that it is
addressed to Congress, a treaty is presumed to be self-
executing.[231]

The Supreme Court has not directly decided whether the
Geneva Convention is self-executing, but it has specified the
required analysis. "The interpretation of a treaty, like the
interpretation of a statute, begins with its text. Because a
treaty ratified by the United States is an agreement among
sovereign powers, [the court has] also considered as aids to
its interpretation the negotiation and drafting history of the
treaty as well as the postratification understanding of signatory
nations."[232] This is in some ways a challenging statement
when applied (as the Supreme Court proceeded to apply it) to
the question of a treaty's domestic status, because different
states use different domestic mechanisms to adhere to their
treaty obligations. International law is largely concerned with
results rather than with methods.[233]

Part 4.1 above discussed the relevant text and history of the
Geneva Convention, particularly articles 1, 6, and 8.[234] Article
1 states in part that no party "shall be required to extend the
benefit of the provisions of this Convention to any motor
vehicle or trailer, or to any driver having remained within its
territory for a continuous period exceeding one year."[235] This
provision, on its face, indicates that the parties recognized that

the treaty would benefit individuals. In no way does this recognition compel a conclusion that the Convention is self-executing, but it does suggest that the treaty is of a type that the Senate might have understood to be directly enforceable.

Article 6 provides that each party "shall take appropriate measures to ensure the observance of the rules set out in" chapter II.[236] This language might be read as evidence that no party intended to give direct domestic effect to those rules or that the Senate, in consenting to ratification, reasonably discerned such intent. However, as explained above, article 6 actually clarifies that each individual rule violation is not necessarily a treaty violation.[237] It does not and need not specify the particular status of the Convention within a state's domestic law. Although the Convention obligates a party to enforce rules of the road that are consistent with those in chapter II, the source of those domestic rules could include existing statutes, new statutes, incorporation of the treaty itself, or any number of other possibilities. With respect to the United States, it was "not anticipated that ... acceptance of the convention will require any changes in motor vehicle laws in this country, nor will it entail any additional expense to public authorities."[238]

Article 8, and indeed all of the rules of the road contained in chapter II, are mandatory in tone and specific as to audience. Then ten substantive articles of chapter II (excluding article 6) use the word "shall" 46 times,[239] and most impose duties directly on "the driver."[240] While some of the rules "are necessarily of an 'admonitory' nature and undoubtedly present difficulties in enforcement,"[241] the same might well be said of provisions within the vehicle codes enacted by the various US states.[242]

Courts appear to generally assume that the Geneva Convention is a source of US law. In his Medellin dissent, Justice Breyer noted that the Geneva Convention's provisions regarding the "rights and obligations of drivers" "are of the sort that this Court has found self-executing,"[243] an observation that the majority did not address. *Schofield v. Hertz Corporation* expressly states, in regard to the Geneva Convention, that "[c]ourts of this state must take judicial notice of all treaties or conventions and they predominate over any statutory provision of the State of Georgia or private guidelines."[244] And *State v. Campos* describes the Geneva Convention as an "exemption" from Ohio's licensing statute.[245]

Furthermore, the US Department of State also considers the Convention to be binding on US states. In response to an inquiry by the US state of Georgia regarding the application of the treaty to foreign nationals who had entered or remained in the United States without authority, the department responded in part that:

> we believe that the State of Georgia, consistent with the [Convention on Road Traffic ("CRT")], (1) must permit an alien to drive in Georgia using a foreign driver's license issued by a country party to the CRT only if the alien has been lawfully admitted to the United States; (2) must permit a lawfully admitted alien to drive in Georgia using a foreign driver's license of a CRT party only during the first year after the alien's admission; and (3) may, in accordance with Georgia's residency laws, require an alien resident in Georgia to obtain a Georgia driver's license as a condition for continued authorization to drive. By the same token, nothing in the CRT would prevent the State of Georgia from applying more liberal rules with respect to the driving privileges of aliens.[246]

For these reasons, it is likely that courts will continue to treat the Geneva Convention as self-executing. Nonetheless, a court might conclude that, with respect to section II's rules of the road, the governmental obligation is merely to "take appropriate measures" and that such an obligation is too vague to be enforced judicially.[247]

4.5.3.3   Not Every Plaintiff Would Have Standing to Invoke Article 8

A party lacks standing to initiate legal action "if it does not have an actual and substantial interest in, or would not be benefited or harmed by, the ultimate outcome of an action."[248] Accordingly, a person who wished to challenge governmental action as contrary to the Geneva Convention would need to demonstrate that automated vehicles had caused or were soon to cause her harm. Taxi drivers, truck drivers, and others whose livelihoods were immediately threatened might satisfy this requirement. However, a court may also conclude that these plaintiffs are not entitled to the protections of the Convention, particularly since the United States is not "required to extend the benefit of the provisions of this Convention to any motor vehicle or trailer, or to any driver having remained within its territory for a continuous period exceeding one year."[249]

4.5.3.4   Domestic Application of the Convention Is Constitutional

When Congress seeks to impose particular requirements for the noncommercial use of highways (such as maximum lawful blood alcohol content or, in the past, maximum lawful speed),[250] it tends to do so through the power of the purse—in this case, the rather large purse that is the federal transportation fund. This context may prompt some uncertainty about the extent of federal power in this area, particularly if the Supreme Court turns toward a more narrow view of Congressional authority.[251] However, under the court's precedent, the federal government can use its treaty power as a means to ends that it could not reach through its other powers.[252]

4.5.4 Certain Domestic Responses to the Convention Are Possible

Even if the Geneva Convention is self-executing, its domestic status remains vulnerable. Congress and the president each have some power over the domestic application of treaties. Under the last-in-time rule, Congress could negate the domestic effect of the treaty by enacting legislation that is irreconcilably inconsistent with it—although this would also place the United States in breach of its international obligations.[253] In contrast, the president could cause the United States to denounce the treaty pursuant to article 32;[254] this would both relieve the United States of its international obligations and, arguably, negate the treaty's domestic effect.[255]

US states have less direct power. Although their actions could have the practical effect of placing the United States in breach of its international obligations,[256] these actions would alter neither the domestic nor the international status of the treaty's provisions. However, by establishing good-faith practice, US states could shape how these provisions are interpreted at the domestic and international levels. For example, a legislature that expressly authorizes automated vehicles might:

> hereby find[] that operation of automated vehicles under the conditions prescribed herein is consistent with article 8 of the Convention on Road Traffic because (1) such operation has the potential to significantly improve highway safety, one of the objects of the Convention; (2) this State shall make such operation reasonably knowable to the foreign visitors contemplated by the Convention; (3) the Convention implicitly permits indirect control over vehicles and animals; (4) there shall remain a driver of each vehicle who shall be able to specify or accept the parameters of operation; and (5) these

parameters shall be consistent with the traffic laws of this State.[257]

State attorneys general, the US state department's office of legal counsel, and other domestic legal actors that undertake to interpret the Geneva Convention might reasonably reach a similar conclusion. This paper now turns to one of these actors, namely the National Highway Traffic Safety Administration.

5   Federal Motor Vehicle Safety Standards Do Not Categorically Prohibit Automated Driving

The National Highway Traffic Safety Administration (NHTSA) regulates the performance of motor vehicles in part through the promulgation and enforcement of rules,[258] including the performance-based[259] standards to which manufacturers, importers, and distributors must certify their new vehicles.[260]

Neither these Federal Motor Vehicle Safety Standards (FMVSSs) nor NHTSA's other rules appear to directly preclude the sale or importation of automated vehicles.[261] These rules, for example, assume but do not expressly require the presence of a driver[262] (defined as "the occupant of a motor vehicle seated immediately behind the steering control system"[263]), do not categorically prohibit drive-by-wire-systems,[264] require no specific description of the technology in a vehicle identification number (VIN),[265] and impose no event data recording (EDR) requirements[266] that would uniquely burden automated vehicles.[267] Similarly, automated vehicles that were designed for particular low-speed applications might fall under NHTSA's less demanding low-speed vehicle standard.[268]

FMVSS 108, however, may be a source of two potential complications, particularly in light of the agency's strikingly conservative approach to this lighting standard.[269] This detailed rule requires a motor vehicle to be equipped with a "vehicular hazard warning signal operating unit" that conforms to the January 1966 version of SAE Recommended Practice J910.[270] That document in turn defines "vehicular hazard warning signal operating unit" as a "driver controlled device which causes all turn signal lamps to flash simultaneously to indicate to the approaching drivers the presence of a vehicular hazard."[271] On at least three occasions, NHTSA has advised that the phrase "driver controlled" precludes automatic activation of hazard flashers.[272]

This is a curious interpretation for two reasons. First, it implies that drivers do not, for example, "control" their brakes, since antilock service brakes are not exclusively "activated and deactivated by the driver."[273] Second, the actual standard distinguishes between the flashers and their operating unit, which suggests that the flashers might be automatically actuated even if the operating unit is not.[274] That is, the "vehicular hazard warning signal operating unit" defined in SAE J910 is only one part of an entire vehicular hazard warning signal system that also includes flashers (covered by SAE J945)[275] and turn signal lamps (covered by SAE J1395).[276] An automatic controller need not supplant the manually switchable operating unit; it could merely provide a second method of actuating the flashers (and therefore a third method of actuating the turn signals). If that controller performs appropriately, it need not "impair[] the effectiveness of" the required equipment.[277]

FMVSS 108 also provides that "[n]o additional lamp, reflective device or other motor vehicle equipment shall be installed that impairs the effectiveness of lighting equipment required by this standard."[278] Because the LiDAR ("light detection and ranging") devices used on some automated vehicles are arguably lamps (since they emit light, whether visible or not) and certainly motor vehicle equipment, NHTSA may apply its strict interpretation of FMVSS 108 to these devices as well. NHTSA has previously taken a cautiously permissive approach to certain laser devices projecting in the visible spectrum.[279]

In addition to specifying particular performance standards, NHTSA imposes specific obligations on an entity that alters a vehicle. In particular, "[w]ith respect to the vehicle alterations it performs, an alterer: (1) Has a duty to determine continued conformity of the altered vehicle with applicable Federal motor vehicle safety, Bumper, and Theft Prevention standards, and (2) Assumes legal responsibility for all duties and liabilities for certification under the Vehicle Safety Act."[280] The conversion of a conventional motor vehicle to an automated vehicle would constitute an alteration if the changes are significant and made before the vehicle is first sold to a consumer.[281]

Furthermore, an automated vehicle that presents an "unreasonable risk" of crashes, death, or injury[282] would impose obligations on NHTSA as well as on the relevant manufacturer and its dealers.[283] In chief, the manufacturer would be independently obligated to provide notice of and a remedy for such a defect,[284] NHTSA would otherwise be required to order that manufacturer to do so,[285] and a dealer would be prohibited from selling a vehicle that remains defective.[286]

Such a vehicle could be defective even if it complies with NHTSA's performance standards. The statutory provisions governing recalls apply to vehicles and equipment that "contain[] a defect related to motor vehicle safety" as well as those that "do[] not comply with an applicable motor vehicle safety standard."[287] A defect "includes any defect in performance, construction, a component, or material of a motor vehicle or motor vehicle equipment,"[288] and motor vehicle safety "means the performance of a motor vehicle or motor vehicle equipment in a way that protects the public against unreasonable risk of accidents occurring because of the design, construction, or performance of a motor vehicle, and against unreasonable risk of death or injury in an accident, and includes nonoperational safety of a motor vehicle."[289]

Finally, rules promulgated by other agencies may also be relevant. The Federal Communications Commission regulates the electromagnetic spectrum, parts of which may be used or affected by automated vehicles.[290] The Federal Motor Carrier Safety Administration regulates commercial trucking.[291] And, depending on the extent of governmental involvement,[292] certain research that involves human subjects may be regulated under a federal policy for the protection of human subjects.[293] These examples, while outside this paper's scope, illustrate the range of federal law potentially implicated by automated vehicles. Relevant state law, to which this paper now turns, is similarly expansive.

6   State Vehicle Codes Do Not Categorically Prohibit Automated Driving

This section surveys the statutory vehicle codes of every US state plus the Uniform Vehicle Code and a selection of other domestic codes. It also reviews some of the case law related to these codes, though by no means comprehensively. It generally does not consider administrative agency rules or practices implementing vehicle codes. And it looks at relevant ordinances in only a tiny fraction of US municipalities.[294]

Because of the broad way in which the term and others like it are defined, an automated vehicle probably has a human "driver."[295] Obligations imposed on that person may limit the independence with which the vehicle may lawfully operate.[296] In addition, the automated vehicle itself must meet numerous requirements, some of which may also complicate its operation.[297] Although three states have expressly established the legality of automated vehicles under certain conditions, their respective laws do not resolve many of the questions raised in this section.[298] Other states that wish to address the question of legality might consider the draft provisions provided as an initial basis for eventual legislation.[299]

6.1   An Automated Vehicle Probably Has a Driver

Unlike the Geneva Convention, no state statute expressly requires that a vehicle have a driver. However, state vehicle codes do variously impose obligations on a vehicle's "driver," "operator," or "owner" or on any "person" who "drive[s]" or "operate[s]" or has "actual physical control of" that vehicle. They also establish certain vehicle requirements that similarly reference the "driver" or "operator." These provisions raise the threshold question of whether an automated vehicle has any such person or persons—and, if so, whom.

"Driver" is a broad concept[300]—so much so that, at least textually, even nonhuman persons can be drivers.[301] In addition, an owner who is not driving her vehicle may nonetheless be responsible for it.[302] This expansive view of responsibility suggests that various persons could be deemed to operate an automated vehicle.[303]

6.1.1   "Driver" Is a Broad Concept

"Driver" and "operator" are broad terms that, in general, refer to anyone who "drives," "operates," or "is in actual physical control of" a vehicle.[304] These three descriptors, which form a vexing Venn diagram that shifts by jurisdiction, collectively encompass a wide range of circumstances. In California, for example, "drivers" have included a person who was exiting her vehicle from the front left seat,[305] a person who failed to engage the parking brake before exiting the vehicle,[306] a person who was towing an occupied vehicle,[307] and a person who was manually pushing an inoperable vehicle owned by an acquaintance.[308] Indeed, a vehicle can simultaneously have multiple drivers.[309]

Definitions of the individual terms, however, create a thicket of inconsistency and logical impossibility.[310] As Maryland's high court observed, "[t]he legislature's definition of 'drive' as meaning, among other things, 'to drive,' unquestionably engenders some confusion"[311]—especially since "drive" also includes "operate," which in turn means "drive,"[312] even though "operating" had been (and perhaps still is) interpreted more broadly than "driving."[313]

And that is just one state. Jurisdictions—whether by statute or through case law—define these terms differently: Whereas California distinguishes between driving (as sometimes requiring some motion) and operating (as not),[314] Illinois probably does not.[315] And jurisdictions also employ the terms differently: While New York directs that "[n]o person shall operate a motor vehicle unless such person is restrained by a safety belt,"[316] Colorado requires that "every driver ... shall wear a fastened safety belt while the motor vehicle is being operated on a street or highway in this state."[317]

The significance of these adventures in connotation depends in part on the interpretive methods that a court applies to the provisions at issue. Courts have occasionally favored practical import over linguistic nuance.[318] Nonetheless, the fiction that statutes contain no superfluous language[319] has led to valiant efforts to distinguish between "driving" and "actual physical control." Accordingly, a person in "actual physical control of" a vehicle can be its "driver" even if she does not "drive" it,[320] and a person who "drives" a vehicle can be a "driver" even if she is not in "actual physical control."[321]

Consider, for example, the question of whether an intoxicated person commits drunk driving by "sleeping it off" in her stationary vehicle.[322] Some courts have asked whether the safety goals behind a drunk-driving prohibition are better served by a construction that discourages drivers from drinking or by one that discourages drunks from driving,[323] and some have looked to whether the statute at issue refers to driving, operating, or actual physical control.[324] So how do these terms compare?

"Drive" is generally defined broadly by legislatures[325] and narrowly by courts.[326] The Uniform Vehicle Code defines the term as "to operate or be in physical control of a vehicle," and the statutory definitions of general application take a similar approach.[327] Wisconsin provides a useful statutory formulation of the "common law definition"[328]: "Drive," for the purpose of that state's drunk-driving law, "means the exercise of physical control over the speed and direction of a motor vehicle *while it is in motion*."[329] The requirement of vehicular movement, in the words of California's high court, captures the "plain meaning"[330] that corresponds to "everyday usage."[331]

"Operate," in turn, has also been defined by legislatures[332] and by courts.[333] Vermont provides the broadest statutory definition: "'Operate',' 'operating' or 'operated' as applied to motor vehicles shall include 'drive,' 'driving' and 'driven' and shall also include an attempt to operate, and shall be construed to cover all matters and things connected with the presence and use of motor vehicles on the highway, whether they be in motion or at rest."[334] "Operate" is statutorily defined in Illinois as "[t]o ride in or on, other than as a passenger, use or control in any manner the operation of any device or vehicle,"[335] in Ohio as "to cause or have caused movement of a vehicle,"[336] and in Indiana as "to navigate a vehicle."[337]

Courts also tend to broadly construe the term when interpreting the numerous rules of the road that use it.[338] Operation usually includes inchoate driving,[339] and "some courts have specifically recognized that a person may operate a vehicle without driving it."[340] The high court in Massachusetts explained, presciently for 1928, that "[a] person operates a motor vehicle ... when, in the vehicle, he intentionally does any act or makes use of any mechanical or electrical agency which alone or in sequence will set in motion the motive power of that vehicle."[341] And Michigan's high court has held that, for the purpose of the state's drunk-driving statute, "once a person using a motor vehicle as a motor vehicle has put the vehicle in motion, or in a position posing a significant risk of causing a collision, such a person continues to operate it until the vehicle is returned to a position posing no such risk."[342]

These broad definitions suggest that a person who is not physically proximate to either a vehicle or the vehicle's driving mechanism might nonetheless "operate" it.[343] However, there may be a limit to this attenuation. In particular, while a person can "operate" a vehicle through limited machine agency,[344] she generally cannot do so through full human agency.[345] While recognizing that "operate" has different meanings in other contexts,[346] New York's high court discerned "a definite meaning" in the Highway Law:

> The word 'operate' is used throughout the statute as signifying a personal act in working the mechanism of the car. The driver operates the car for the owner, but the owner does not operate the car unless he drives it himself. If the meaning were extended to include an owner acting either by himself or by agents or employees, the provisions of the Highway Law would be replete with repetitious jargon.[347]

"Actual physical control" can be broader than operation but probably does involve physical presence. Under the classic definition first proffered by Montana's high court, a person is in actual physical control of a motor vehicle if she "has existing or present bodily restraint, directing influence, domination or regulation, of" it.[348] Florida juries are told that "'[a]ctual physical control' of a motor vehicle means the defendant must be physically in or on the vehicle and have the capability to operate the vehicle, regardless of whether [he] [she] is actually operating the vehicle at the time."[349] Where the phrase is used in drunk-driving statutes, some states provide a precise definition,[350] while others ask juries to consider the "totality of the circumstances"[351] with a view toward establishing whether the defendant "actually posed a threat to the public by the exercise of actual control over it while impaired."[352]

That, then, is a driver. Importantly, this paper does not attempt to distinguish among these various terms or to trace their specific usage in individual statutory provisions. Even though the particular wording of a particular statute in a particular state may matter to the particular court applying it to the particular facts of a particular case, the reader may find such an immense undertaking to be neither particularly interesting nor particularly illuminating. Instead, this paper broadly uses driver as shorthand for any statutory references to drivers, operators, persons who drive or operate vehicles, and any other related concepts. The remainder of this section proceeds from this stipulation to consider, generally, who those persons might be and what obligations they may have.

6.1.2   Nonhuman Persons Can Technically Be Drivers

On a literal reading of many vehicle codes, those persons may not even need to be human. More than half of states expressly include firms, corporations, partnerships, and other legal entities within the meaning of "person."[353] Although such a definition appears as early as 1926,[354] its original rationale is not entirely clear. Indeed, only a few scattered statutes refer to the operation of vehicles by persons other than humans.[355] This quirk may actually make sense in the context of automated vehicles.[356] For now, however, charging a corporation with reckless driving or negligent homicide may be conceivable[357] but is not likely[358] and in any case lacks known precedent. The best explanation for these definitions is also the reason why treating a corporation as a driver is generally unnecessary: Vehicle owners need not be natural persons, and as the next section describes, they might be liable for their vehicles even if they are not driving them.

6.1.3   Vehicle Owners May Be Responsible for Their Vehicles

A brief but important aside: To varying degrees, states impose criminal or quasicriminal liability on owners who permit others to drive their vehicles.[359] In Washington, "[b]oth a person operating a vehicle with the express or implied permission of the owner and the owner of the vehicle are responsible for any act or omission that is declared unlawful in this chapter. The primary responsibility is the owner's."[360] Some states permit an inference that the owner of a vehicle was its operator for certain offenses;[361] Wisconsin provides what is by far the most detailed statutory set of rebuttable presumptions.[362] Many others punish owners who knowingly permit their vehicles to be driven unlawfully.[363] Although these owners are not drivers, they are assumed to exercise some judgment or control with respect to those drivers—an instance of vicarious liability that suggests an owner of an automated vehicle might be liable for merely permitting its automated operation.[364]

6.1.4   Various Persons Could Be an Automated Vehicle's Driver

These expansive definitions suggest that even an automated vehicle probably has a driver—and quite possibly multiple drivers—under existing state law. The driver determination will ultimately depend on the particular technology, jurisdiction, and statutory provision at issue. However, in a highly generalized descriptive sense, any person who directly commands a vehicle to perform some act or omission likely qualifies as its driver with respect both to that act or omission and to the consequences that follow proximately from it. "Directly commands" implies that the person issues specific instructions without any human intermediary.[365] It also implies that the person has the means to issue these instructions and some degree of culpability in their issuance. This definition applies to natural persons and might apply to corporate persons.

On the human side, physical presence would likely continue to provide a proxy for or presumption of driving.[366] In other words, an individual who is physically positioned to provide real-time input to a motor vehicle may well be treated as its driver. This is particularly likely at levels of automation that involve human input for certain portions of a trip.

In addition, an individual who starts or dispatches an automated vehicle, who initiates the automated operation of that vehicle, or who specifies certain parameters of operation probably qualifies as a driver under existing law. That individual may use some device—anything from a physical key to the click of a mouse to the sound of her voice—to activate the vehicle by herself. She may likewise deliberately request that the vehicle assume the active driving task. And she may set the vehicle's maximum speed or level of assertiveness.

This working definition is unclear in the same ways that existing law is likely to be unclear. Relevant acts might occur at any level of the primary driving task, from a decision to take a particular trip to a decision to exceed any speed limit by ten miles per hour.[367] A tactical decision like speeding is closely connected with the consequences—whether a moving violation or an injury—that may result. But treating an individual who dispatches her fully automated vehicle as the driver for the entirety of the trip could attenuate the relationship between legal responsibility and legal fault.[368] Nonetheless, strict liability of this sort is accepted within tort law[369] and present, however controversially, in US criminal law.[370] It is often connected with a generalized rather than a particularized notion of control—the control exercised by a vehicle owner over her vehicle,[371] the control exercised by a pet owner over her pet,[372] the control exercised by an employer over its employees,[373] and the control exercised by an executive over her company.[374] It is also common for infractions that are considered minor, including many traffic violations.[375] In this sense, perhaps it is "significant" that driver is often defined as "one 'who drives' as distinguished from one 'who is driving.'"[376]

The scope of a command may also be unclear. This uncertainty is related in part to the difference between instructions and data. Consider a personal rapid transit system consisting of pods that can each transport several passengers on demand around a public campus. Does the passenger actively instruct the vehicle to drive when she requests a pick-up or presses the "go" button upon entering? Or is she merely indicating to the vehicle that she is ready to be driven? In the same way, is a police officer who waves an automated vehicle into a detour instructing that vehicle or merely providing an environmental input? And is a human who tampers with a vehicle's automated functionality commanding the vehicle?

On the corporate side, a firm that designs or supplies a vehicle's automated functionality or that provides data or other digital services might qualify as a driver under existing law. The key element, as provided in the working definition, may be the lack of a human intermediary: A human who provides some input may still seem a better fit for a human-centered vehicle code than a company with other relevant legal exposure. However, as noted above, public outrage is another element that may motivate new uses of existing laws.[377]

A person's status as driver might become a mixed question of law and fact that is resolved categorically or contextually. A categorical approach would fix the identity of the driver largely ex ante: Some class of natural or corporate person—the one who sits in the driver's seat, initiates automated operation, owns the vehicle, or provides the automation system, for example—would be deemed to drive some class of automated vehicle. Regulators in Nevada and legislators in Florida and California have already taken this approach,[378] and judges anywhere could as well. Conversely, a contextual approach would determine the identity of the driver largely ex post: The human or corporate person or persons with a causal connection to a particular, and probably unlawful or tortious, driving behavior would be the driver or drivers. In an easy case, the person who instructs an automated vehicle to exceed the speed limit might be the effective driver for the purpose of a prohibition against speeding. If that same vehicle fails to reduce its speed during a blizzard, the manufacturer might be its effective driver.[379]

It is also possible than an automated vehicle could actually have no driver for the purpose of a particular statutory provision. The sections that follow consider a number of provisions that may on their face be inapposite to automated vehicles. In California, for example, "[n]o person shall drive upon any highway any vehicle designed or used for" transporting people or freight for more than a certain number of hours in a certain period.[380] Applying this provision with respect to an automated vehicle that operates without any human presence may be like charging a building owner with the violation of wage and hour laws for running the building's elevators 24 hours a day without pay.[381] In contrast, a far less plausible claim would be that a prohibition on speeding does not apply to an automated vehicle because no "person" is driving it.[382]

The vehicle itself is not a driver under existing law. While wholly speculative, this approach—granting legal personhood to robots—is nonetheless intriguing. It is notable that an early draft of Nevada's pertinent regulation provided that "[i]f a driver is not required, the autonomous technology shall be granted all of the rights and shall be subject to all of the duties applicable to the driver of a vehicle, except those provisions which by their nature can have no application."[383] The practical effect of such a provision might be to put more legal pressure on the vehicle owner, who might be treated as the vehicle's principal.[384]

Finally, a caution: Identifying the driver is hardly dispositive for the purpose of product liability, as an automated vehicle may be defective even if a human remains the sole legal driver. The rules of the road may establish standards to which retailers, manufacturers, and suppliers are held,[385] and companies can also be liable for the foreseeable misuse of their products.[386] Conversely, passengers may bear some responsibility for the operation of the vehicles in which they ride.[387] These limited observations, while beyond the scope of this paper, nonetheless demonstrate that the question of who drives an automated vehicle is only the beginning of the legal analysis. On the assumption that this question is answerable, the next section considers the obligations of an automated vehicle's driver.

6.2   Drivers Must Act Safely

Whoever or whatever drives an automated vehicle has certain obligations; these obligations in turn may determine how and by whom any such vehicle may lawfully be used. As discussed above, a person is likely to be identified as the driver of an automated vehicle. Accordingly, even though the statutes in this section do not expressly require a driver, there is likely to be some person connected to the vehicle who must be licensed,[388] who may need to be physically present,[389] and who must act prudently.[390]

Furthermore, offenses like driving without a license, permitting operation by a person without a license, leaving a vehicle without engaging its brakes, driving with an obstructed view, driving recklessly, or operating an unsafe vehicle may prove appealing to a government agency trying to discourage automated vehicles or to an attorney trying to establish negligence in the operation of such a vehicle.

6.2.1   Drivers Must Be Licensed

A person without a valid driving license can generally be a driver or operator—simply not a lawful one. In California, for example, "[a] person may not drive a motor vehicle upon a highway, unless the person then holds a valid driver's license issued under this code."[391] Indeed, "[n]o owner of a motor vehicle may knowingly allow another person to drive the vehicle upon a highway unless the owner determines that the person possesses a valid driver's license that authorizes the person to operate the vehicle."[392]

To receive a California driver's license, a person must provide certain identifying information, be of legal age, have satisfactory corrected eyesight, understand signs and signals, possess a "reasonable knowledge" of the rules of the road, be able to "safely operate a motor vehicle upon a highway," and meet other requirements.[393] However, "[a] physical defect of the applicant that, in the opinion of the department, is compensated for to ensure safe driving ability, shall not prevent the issuance of a license to the applicant."[394]

The mechanism by which someone other than a human would obtain a driving license is unclear. For example, some companies may possess great vision, but "a test of the applicant's eyesight" may nonetheless be difficult.[395] And while General Motors may (or may not)[396] meet a state's minimum age requirement, Google would not.[397]

Automated vehicles could lead to changes in these licensing requirements to the benefit of disabled persons or, conceivably, corporate persons. A state department of motor vehicles might determine that certain disabilities do not prevent the safe operation of an automated vehicle,[398] a state legislature might amend the relevant statutory provisions, or a person denied a license might challenge those provisions or their application as a violation of the state or federal constitution (particularly due process or equal protection guarantees) or the federal Americans with Disabilities Act (ADA).[399] As the sections that follow describe, however, a license is just the beginning.

6.2.2   Drivers May Need to Be Present

No statute expressly requires that a motor vehicle's operator must be physically present in the vehicle. To the contrary, the ordinary definition of the broader term "vehicle" is inconsistent with any such requirement: Trailers and semitrailers, which are typically designed for cargo rather than people, qualify as vehicles,[400] and some states even prohibit riding in house trailers while they are being moved.[401] Depending on the jurisdiction and the context, however, these towed vehicles may or may not qualify as "motor vehicles,"[402] which generally means "a vehicle that is self-propelled."[403]

Regardless, a number of rules either imply that physical presence is required or make compliance without such presence impractical. These rules fall into seven rough categories: unattended vehicles, abandoned vehicles, crash obligations, safety belts, driver sight, driver interference, and "control." With the exception of particular rules regarding "control," they are also quite common and fairly consistent. Depending on the extent of automation and the identity of the driver, their application to this person may be clear and reasonable, clear but absurd, or—in the case of a nonhuman driver—wholly metaphysical.[404]

The most conspicuous provisions are those relating to unattended vehicles. The formulation in California, which is similar to that in many other states, specifies that "[n]o person driving, or in control of, or in charge of, a motor vehicle shall permit it to stand on any highway unattended without first effectively setting the brakes thereon and stopping the motor thereof."[405] Other states also require the operator to stop the engine and remove the key from the ignition[406]—or even from the vehicle.[407] And the Navajo Nation specifies that "[a]ll reasonable precautions ... be taken to prevent the movement of any vehicle left unattended."[408] These provisions, however, are presumably directed at more conventionally "driverless"[409] vehicles. Automated vehicles might well be permanently "attended" by computers, companies, or remote humans, and a literal construction of many of these provisions would not necessarily prohibit a vehicle from automatically disengaging its brakes and keylessly resuming motion after its driver's departure.

Some statutes relating to abandoned vehicles may pose similarly surmountable textual obstacles. In Washington, for example, "[i]t is unlawful for the operator of a vehicle to leave the vehicle unattended within the limits of any highway unless the operator of the vehicle arranges for the prompt removal of the vehicle."[410] Vehicles "left unattended" on Illinois freeways may be removed after only two hours.[411] And "any peace officer who discovers a motor vehicle which has been left unattended on a public" highway in Georgia shall "immediately" perform a safety check.[412]

Other requirements may be difficult for a remote driver to satisfy. Drivers typically have certain obligations following serious crashes, including immediately stopping and remaining at or near the scene to provide contact information and, in some cases, to render aid to the injured.[413] And drivers of certain vehicles are required to "listen" when crossing a railroad track.[414]

An operator removed from a vehicle may even be obliged to buckle up—at least textually. In Ohio, for example, "[e]ach driver and passenger of a motor vehicle operated on a street or highway in this State shall wear a properly adjusted and fastened seat safety belt."[415] Given the broad definitions of both "driver" and "operate,"[416] literal constructions of such provisions could produce absurd results on highways today: A vehicle's driver may experience some difficulty exiting her vehicle with her seatbelt securely fastened. However, while this suggests the need for a flexible interpretation of the provision, it does not dictate the result of that interpretation in the context of an automated vehicle.

Although a human driver's mere physical (and belted) presence in a vehicle would satisfy these four issues, more may be required. Take the particular example of mirror requirements found in most states. In Ohio, "[o]perators of vehicles ... shall have a clear and unobstructed view to the front and to both sides of their vehicles ... and shall have a clear view to the rear."[417] And in Washington, "[e]very motor vehicle shall be equipped with a mirror mounted on the left side of the vehicle and so located to reflect to the driver a view of the highway for a distance of at least two hundred feet to the rear."[418] A vehicle with a human driver seated in the rear may not comply with a literal construction of these provisions.

Similarly, most states have adopted some variant of the rule that "[n]o person shall drive a vehicle when it is so loaded, or when there are in the front seat such number of persons as to obstruct the view of the driver to the front or sides of the vehicle or as to interfere with the driver's control over the driving mechanism of the vehicle."[419] While this requirement would not, under a literal construction, preclude a backseat driver, it both reflects the assumption that a driver is able to see and introduces the difficult question of "control" in the context of state law.

Notably, these provisions refer to "control" rather than "actual physical control." As noted above, that longer term appears frequently in definitions of "driver" and "operator" as well as in prohibitions of drunk driving.[420] In light of the canon, however absurd, that legislatures choose their words carefully,[421] this is an important distinction. It suggests that "control over the driving mechanism," just like the "control" required by the Geneva Convention, need not be actual, physical, or actually physical.

A significant exception is New York. One provision states, somewhat innocuously, that "[e]very motor vehicle, operated or driven upon the public highways of the state, shall be provided with adequate brakes and steering mechanism in good working order and sufficient to control such vehicle at all times when the same is in use."[422] But a more striking provision directs that "[n]o person shall operate a motor vehicle without having at least one hand or, in the case of a physically handicapped person, at least one prosthetic device or aid on the steering mechanism at all times when the motor vehicle is in motion."[423] In other words, an automated vehicle in New York would need to quite literally steer its human driver.

New York may be the only state with such a categorical statutory requirement. Massachusetts provides that "[n]o person, when operating a motor vehicle, shall permit to be on or in the vehicle or on or about his person anything which may interfere with or impede the proper operation of the vehicle or any equipment by which the vehicle is operated or controlled, except that a person may operate a motor vehicle while using a ... 2-way radio or mobile telephone [except as otherwise provided] as long as 1 hand remains on the steering wheel at all times."[424] And Puerto Rico directs that "[n]o person shall operate a vehicle, carriage or motorcycle, carrying packages or other objects that prevent him/her from keeping both hands on the bridle or handlebars simultaneously."[425] These requirements, however, do not apply to regular driving—unless regular driving now involves a cell phone.[426]

"Control" is susceptible to a much broader array of meanings. Some uses are clearly abstract; Michigan, for example, prohibits a person from "knowingly authoriz[ing] or permit[ting] a motor vehicle owned by him or under his control to be driven in violation of" the vehicle code,[427] and Texas restricts where a person may "move a vehicle that is not lawfully under [her] control."[428]

Others are somewhat more concrete. New Jersey's unattended vehicle provision, unlike those quoted above, states that a "person who leaves a motor vehicle, with its engine running, stationary on the highway and unoccupied by a person able to control it, and without setting the hand brake in such manner as to prevent the vehicle from moving, shall be fined not less than ten nor more than twenty-five dollars for each offense."[429] An unrelated provision in North Carolina directs that "[t]he steering mechanism of every self-propelled motor vehicle operated on the highway shall be maintained in good working order, sufficient to enable the operator to control the vehicle's movements and to maneuver it safely."[430] And Ohio requires drivers to "be[] in reasonable control" of their motor vehicles.[431]

These three uses of control evoke the Geneva Convention's requirement that "[d]rivers shall at all times be able to control their vehicles."[432] And, like article 8, though these provisions could refer to the physical manipulation of a vehicle's driving mechanisms, their primary objective is the safe operation of that vehicle vis-à-vis other road users. This primary objective may or may not be satisfied by a particular automated vehicle. But if it is,[433] then a reasonable interpretation of these ambiguous provisions would not extend them beyond their literal requirements.[434] Control in this sense becomes an obligation of prudence, to which this paper now turns.

6.2.3 Drivers Must Act Prudently

Within most jurisdictions, diverse statutes collectively impose on drivers what might be called an obligation of prudence.[435] This obligation has two overlapping aspects. The first focuses on the driver in her vehicle: Is she exercising responsibility for the task of driving? Is she distracted or impaired in any other way? The second focuses on the vehicle in its environment: Is it speeding or swerving? Is it disposed to cause a crash—or has it already? This dual focus is often present in the specific rules that demand prudence—in their enforcement if not in their formulation.

Foremost among these rules is the common prohibition against reckless driving, typically defined as "driv[ing] in willful or wanton disregard for the safety of persons or property."[436] "[T]he offense of reckless driving contains three distinct elements: (1) the conscious and intentional operation of a motor vehicle, (2) in a manner which creates an unreasonable risk of harm to others, (3) where such risk is or should be known to the driver."[437] A person can commit reckless driving by operating a vehicle that she knows to be in an unsafe condition;[438] Virginia expressly provides that a "person shall be guilty of reckless driving who drives a vehicle which is not under proper control or which has inadequate or improperly adjusted brakes on any highway in the Commonwealth."[439]

A number of states additionally punish driving that is careless or negligent but not reckless. Persons in Florida and Louisiana are to drive "in a careful and prudent manner."[440] And in New Jersey, "[n]otwithstanding any other provision of law to the contrary, it shall be unlawful for any person to drive or operate a motor vehicle in an unsafe manner likely to endanger a person or property."[441] That state further provides that "[a] person who drives a vehicle carelessly, or without due caution and circumspection, in a manner so as to endanger, or be likely to endanger, a person or property, shall be guilty of careless driving."[442]

Other states also incorporate the notion of "due care" in their codes. In Georgia, "[a] driver shall exercise due care in operating a motor vehicle on the highways of this state and shall not engage in any actions which shall distract such driver from the safe operation of such vehicle." Hawaii prescribes a penalty for operating a vehicle "without due care."[443] Washington specifies that "[c]ompliance with speed requirements ... shall not relieve the operator of any vehicle from the further exercise of due care and caution as further circumstances shall require." Wyoming provides that "[a]ny person who drives any vehicle in a manner inconsistent with the exercise of due and diligent care normally exercised by a reasonably prudent person under similar circumstances and where such operation of a motor vehicle creates an unreasonable risk of harm to other persons or property is guilty of careless driving."[444] And New York, among others, requires drivers to "exercise due care to avoid colliding with any bicyclist, pedestrian, or domestic animal upon any roadway"— an obligation that applies "[n]otwithstanding the provisions of any other law to the contrary."[445]

Oklahoma's vehicle code uniquely specifies that "[t]he operator of every vehicle, while driving, shall devote their full time and attention to such driving."[446] However, "[n]o law enforcement officer shall issue a citation" for the violation of this provision unless she "observes that the operator of the vehicle is involved in an accident or observes the operator of the vehicle driving in such a manner that poses an articulable danger to other persons on the roadway that is not otherwise specified in statute."[447] Tennessee specifies somewhat similar driver requirements, but with more attenuation—and with enough length to consign the full text to the footnote below.[448]

Rather than affirmatively require attentiveness, a few jurisdictions prohibit distraction. A driver in Georgia "shall not engage in any actions which shall distract such driver from the safe operation of such vehicle."[449] In Wisconsin, "[n]o person while driving a motor vehicle shall be so engaged or occupied as to interfere with the safe driving of such vehicle."[450] Arkansas prohibits "any person" from "driv[ing] or operat[ing] any vehicle in such a careless manner as to evidence a failure to keep a proper lookout for other traffic, vehicular or otherwise, or in such a manner as to evidence a failure to maintain proper control."[451] Maine punishes an operator who, while engaged in an activity "[t]hat is not necessary to the operation of the vehicle" and "actually impairs, or would reasonably be expected to impair, [her ability] to safely operate the vehicle," either commits another traffic offense or is involved in a reportable crash.[452] And Washington, D.C. prohibits "distracted driving,"[453] which "means inattentive driving while operating a motor vehicle that results in the unsafe operation of the vehicle where such inattention is caused by reading, writing, performing personal grooming, interacting with pets or unsecured cargo, using personal communications technologies, or engaging in any other activity which causes distractions."[454]

In contrast to these jurisdictions, the majority of states simply restrict (a narrower set of) particular distracting activities. These include bans on the use of video displays visible to the operator for purposes unrelated to driving, conditions on the use of cell phones and other electronic devices, and prohibitions both on interfering with the vehicle's operation and driving during such interference.[455] Oregon and Washington are particularly concerned about drivers "embracing" their passengers.[456] Curiously, few states address actual sleeping; "Maggie's Law" in New Jersey specifies that extreme fatigue may constitute recklessness for the purpose of that state's vehicular homicide law,[457] and Ohio directs that "[n]o person shall drive a 'commercial motor vehicle' ... while [her] ability or alertness is so impaired by fatigue, illness, or other causes that it is unsafe for the person to drive such vehicle."

A driver's actions may constitute civil negligence without reaching the level of criminal culpability.[458] (The terminology is not particularly helpful: A tort action may allege civil negligence; a minor traffic offense may constitute a civil infraction.) The difference in some cases merely goes to the result of the conduct: California, for example, statutorily penalizes generalized negligent driving only if death results.[459] Drivers may therefore have duties of care that extend beyond express statutory directives.[460]

These duties become relevant only if there has been an injury to person or property. In the case of no crash, any related negligence lacks a requisite injury. And in the case of a crash that vigilance could not have prevented, the lack of such vigilance cannot be the cause of the crash, regardless of whether that inattention would constitute negligence as a matter of law.[461] Only in the case of a crash that vigilance would have prevented is the human driver's conduct relevant.

Nonetheless, civil suits alleging driver negligence can inform this broader sense of prudence, particularly with respect to any expectation of vigilance.[462] In its simplest formulation, "the control that is required of a motorist is such as will prevent the collision with another vehicle not being operated negligently."[463] To this end, "drivers are under a duty (1) to maintain a reasonably safe rate of speed; (2) to have their automobiles under reasonable control; (3) to keep a proper lookout, under the circumstances then existing, to see and be aware of what was in their view; and (4) to use reasonable care to avoid an accident."[464] They must "exercise a diligence commensurate with hazards disclosed under surrounding circumstances, and the lookout which ... is ... most effective in the light of all present conditions and those reasonably to be anticipated."[465] The driver is "chargeable with knowledge of what a prudent and vigilant operator would have seen, and is negligent if he fails to discover a vehicle which, or a traveler whom, he could have discovered in time to avoid the injury in the exercise of reasonable care."[466]

These statutory or common law obligations might apply to the human driver of an automated vehicle in at least three ways. The first involves inputs: Depending on actual, perceived, and expected performance of the particular vehicle, the instructions that this human issues to it may be imprudent. For example, dispatching an untested vehicle without supervision might be reckless, even if no harm results. But using a widely accepted technology in the manner intended is unlikely to be considered reckless or even negligent.[467]

The second involves outputs: Particularly with less mainstream technologies, the driver may function as a guarantor of vehicle performance. In this sense, prudence would be measured by what the vehicle actually does in its environment. For example, a driver whose vehicle performs poorly might be driving recklessly.[468] Again, perceptions of the technology may influence expectations, and outcomes that are seen as unforeseeable might not be attributed to the driver.

The third involves vigilance. The key question here is whether a particular state's generalized obligation of vigilance is absolute or contextual. If that obligation is absolute, then the driver must be attentive regardless of the vehicle's performance. If, however, the obligation of vigilance is contextual rather than absolute, then what the driver must do (or cannot do) depends on what the vehicle can do.[469]

A German project group concluded that the German traffic code[470] read in connection with the Vienna Convention on Road Traffic establishes an absolute obligation: The (presumably human) driver must be in control of her vehicle and attentive to her surroundings, regardless of the level of automation.[471] Similarly, state law prohibitions on particular distractions—like watching television—are generally without relevant exception.[472]

In contrast, much of the language in statutes and case law implies a relative approach. "[D]ue care," "safe operation," "proper lookout," and "proper control," for example, beg the question of what is "due," "safe," and "proper."[473] These terms do not provide certainty, but they do imply context. The variation present in the common law duty of due care tends to support this conclusion.[474]

Importantly, this analysis applies to the human driver, not to the automated vehicle: The manufacturer of such a vehicle may be held to a higher standard under product liability law. That issue is beyond this paper's scope. However, it introduces the second prong of the legality analysis: In addition to requiring that human drivers be safe, existing law requires the vehicles they drive to be safe as well.

6.3   Automated Vehicles Must Be Safe

The previous section surveyed relevant obligations currently imposed on human drivers. These obligations extend to automated vehicles in two senses. First, an automated vehicle that is driving imprudently is probably being driven imprudently; in other words, the human driver of an imprudently driving automated vehicle is probably driving imprudently. Second, an automated vehicle that is driving unsafely is likely unsafe. Texas makes this relationship explicit: In its vehicle code, "a reference to an operator includes a reference to the vehicle operated by the operator if the reference imposes a duty or provides a limitation on the movement or other operation of that vehicle."[475] Automated vehicles must satisfy vehicular analogs to the prohibitions on unlicensed and unsafe drivers.[476] They must also comply with rules of the road that were written for humans rather than machines.[477]

6.3.1 Unsafe Vehicles Are Prohibited

The various statutory mechanisms with which states keep "unsafe" motor vehicles off their roadways fall generally into three categories: operation, registration, and modification.[478] Application of these provisions to automated vehicles may depend on both the actual and the perceived performance of these vehicles.[479]

Many states expressly prohibit the operation of dangerous vehicles.[480] In California, "[i]t is unlawful to operate any vehicle or combination of vehicles which is in an unsafe condition, or which is not safely loaded, and which presents an immediate safety hazard."[481] In Texas, it is a misdemeanor to "operate[] or move[] or, as an owner, knowingly permit[] another to operate or move, a vehicle that ... is unsafe so as to endanger a person."[482] Police officers in some states are specifically empowered to order a vehicle's driver "to stop and submit such vehicle to an inspection and any tests as may be appropriate."[483]

Some states explicitly limit the registration of unsafe vehicles. (In general, registration is required for vehicles that are used on highways or other publicly accessible areas.[484]) In California, "registration or the renewal or transfer of registration of a vehicle" may be refused if "the vehicle is mechanically unfit or unsafe to be operated or moved on the highways."[485] In New York, "the commissioner may refuse to register any vehicle or class of vehicles for use on the public highways where he determines that the characteristics of such vehicle or class of vehicles make such vehicle or vehicles unsafe for highway operation."[486] In Massachusetts, the registrar may additionally "suspend or revoke" the registration of an unsafe motor vehicle.[487]

Jurisdictions take a variety of statutory approaches to the modification of vehicles. North Dakota prohibits, with certain exceptions, the operation of a motor vehicle "with alterations or changes from the manufacturer's original design of the suspension, steering, or braking system."[488] California expressly restricts only those modifications that impair vertical clearance.[489] Pennsylvania, Hawaii, and, notably, Nevada require certain modified vehicles to undergo special inspections.[490] Wisconsin prohibits the use of such vehicles to "transport passengers for hire."[491] And Rhode Island specifically criminalizes tampering with a vehicle without the consent of its owner—a provision that could have interesting application if, in the future, a vehicle's software is sabotaged by hackers or remotely updated by its developer.[492] In addition to imposing different requirements, states also define key terms differently: A conventional motor vehicle retrofitted with automation technology is probably a "reconstructed vehicle" in Hawaii but not Pennsylvania.[493]

There are two key points about these provisions. First, they are in one sense the vehicular counterparts to the obligations of prudence imposed on drivers. Whereas a human who drives unreasonably may be committing "reckless driving," a vehicle that does the same may be "unsafe for highway operation." Second, like the prudential requirements, these vehicle requirements depend in large part on administrative discretion, in this case the clerk who determines whether to deny registration to a vehicle or the police officer who decides to pull it over.

6.3.2 Particular Equipment Requirements Apply

Some states have fairly obscure equipment requirements that may at least superficially conflict with potential elements of an automated vehicle's operation. The common mirror requirement discussed above is one such example.[494] Consider three others:

- California prohibits "any lamp or illuminating device not required or permitted in this code."[495] A lamp is a device that emits light.[496] The LiDAR ("light detection and ranging") devices used on some automated vehicles also emit light.[497] Are they prohibited?[498]

- Missouri forbids, with some exceptions, the operation of a motor vehicle or trailer with "any device which emits an electronic message directed to the front, side or rear of the exterior of the vehicle or trailer," including "words, phrases, sentences, numbers and other symbols or combinations thereof."[499] Although this is presumably directed at advertising and other distractions, might it nonetheless limit how an automated vehicle can communicate with human road users?

- Georgia requires that "[o]ne of the means of brake operation shall consist of a mechanical connection from the operating lever to the brake shoes or bands."[500] If this requirement is not precluded by federal safety regulations,[501] what does it mean for future brake-by-wire systems?

These examples are probably not fatal to the legal operation of an automated vehicle that operates safely and stops quickly. But they will, at some point, be considered by someone—whether a legislator, a regulator, a police officer, or a judge—who will have to reconcile the text of these provisions with their presumed intent.

6.3.3 Rules of the Road May Complicate Automated Driving

The rules of the road as codified assume human judgment, and the rules of the road as observed reflect that judgment.

These dependencies may complicate the lawful operation of automated vehicles.

Consider speeding. "It is unlawful for a driver of a vehicle to fail to obey" a posted speed limit,[502] and "[n]o person shall drive a vehicle upon a highway at a speed greater than is reasonable or prudent."[503] These rules are not coextensive: A driver can violate both, one, or neither.[504] Because the first rule is nominally quantitative, determining ex ante the requirements for compliance is generally straightforward. In contrast, because the second rule is nominally qualitative, determining those requirements ex ante may be more difficult.

This quantitative/qualitative distinction is not absolute. A driver might exceed a posted speed limit to comply with another rule or to prevent a concrete harm; a community may condone or even expect minor noncompliance; and the state, acting through budgets, policies, and the discretion of its individual agents, may decline to punish certain prima facie violations. Conversely, a "reasonable and prudent" speed for a given vehicle on a given roadway under given environmental conditions could conceivably be quantified either prescriptively or descriptively. This is already done on a crude level: Nonstatutory speed limits, for example, are often set by reference to the speed at or below which 85 percent of vehicles travel.[505]

Vehicle codes are replete with other rules that are nominally qualitative or absolute. "Reasonable and prudent" may be less demanding than the "extreme caution" required of commercial drivers in certain circumstances.[506] Slow-moving vehicles "shall [generally] be driven in the right-hand lane for traffic or as close as practicable to the right-hand edge or curb," a prescription that does not mean "as close as possible."[507] "No person shall drive upon a highway at such a slow speed as to impede or block the normal and reasonable movement of traffic unless the reduced speed is necessary for safe operation, because of a grade, or in compliance with law."[508]

And "[t]he driver of a vehicle approaching a pedestrian within any marked or unmarked crosswalk shall exercise all due care and shall reduce the speed of the vehicle or take any other action relating to the operation of the vehicle as necessary to safeguard the safety of the pedestrian."[509]

Although these references to reasonableness, prudence, practicability, and due care demonstrate that the law accepts risk at a certain level, they neither specify this level nor prescribe a basis for determining it. That determination may be highly subjective, innately and imperfectly probabilistic, value-laden, and outcome-dependent. Indeed, perceived risk is different than actual risk: Humans tend to inflate some dangers and discount others.[510] These rules are generally not considered unconstitutionally vague,[511] but this hardly means that they are easy to translate into legally defensible code.[512] In other words, application of these laws to automated vehicles may present both design challenges and liability concerns.

Another significant design challenge merits mention: In many states, a person is required to comply with lawful orders or instructions issued by authorized persons, which may include police officers, firefighters, and crossing guards.[513] These instructions, which might be issued orally or physically, may even contravene (and supersede) traffic control devices like signals, stop signs, or lane markings.[514] Although the failure of a person to follow instructions of which she is unaware might not be "willful,"[515] an automated vehicle may not be entitled to obliviousness. In this way, as with other rules discussed, an automated vehicle may be just one part of an essential human-machine system.[516] The next part describes inchoate state efforts to expressly regulate that system.

6.4   Three States Expressly Regulate Automated Vehicles

This part summarizes state laws that expressly address the legality of automated vehicles. Nevada,[517] Florida,[518] and

California[519] have now enacted such laws, and bills are pending in a number of additional jurisdictions.[520] Critically, none of these state laws would prevail in the face of conflicting federal law, including the federal motor vehicle regulations discussed and, to the extent that it is cognizable as federal law, the Geneva Convention. Moreover, these laws do not resolve many of the related issues presented in this paper.[521]

6.4.1   Nevada Conditions the Legality of These Vehicles

In 2011, Nevada became the first state to enact legislation directed at automated vehicles. The primary legislation, passed as Assembly Bill (AB) 511, defines "autonomous vehicle"[522] and directs the state's Department of Motor Vehicles to "adopt regulations authorizing the operation of autonomous vehicles on highways within the State of Nevada."[523] These regulations are to include, inter alia, "minimum safety standards" and a special "driver's license endorsement" that "must, in its restrictions or lack thereof, recognize the fact that a person is not required to actively drive an autonomous vehicle."[524] This language suggests that a driver's license with such an endorsement could be more or less widely available than a normal license.[525]

Separate legislation, passed as Senate Bill (SB) 140, provides that, for the purpose of the state's restrictions on the use of cell phones by drivers, "a person shall be deemed not to be operating a motor vehicle if the motor vehicle is driven autonomously through the use of artificial-intelligence software and the autonomous operation of the motor vehicle is authorized by law."[526] (Notably, the DMV's regulation declines to extend this legal conclusion beyond the context of cell phones.)[527]

The DMV's initial regulation took effect in March 2012.[528] In that regulation, the DMV sought to:

provide[] more clarification to the stakeholders regarding what is not considered autonomous. Self parallel parking and other systems today require some type of human intervention to successfully operate the vehicle. The autonomous vehicle, per Nevada's definition, does not require human intervention to operate the vehicle. There is a clear distinction between the two systems.[529]

Accordingly, the DMV:

will interpret the term "autonomous vehicle" to exclude a vehicle enabled with a safety system or driver assistance system, including, without limitation, a system to provide electronic blind spot assistance, crash avoidance, emergency braking, parking assistance, adaptive cruise control, lane keep assistance, lane departure warnings and traffic jam and queuing assistance, unless the vehicle is also enabled with artificial intelligence and technology that allows the vehicle to carry out all the mechanical operations of driving without the active control or continuous monitoring of a natural person.[530]

Despite this additional clarification, certain potential technologies could arguably fall on either side of this line.[531] Indeed, other states could conceivably interpret similar language differently.[532]

The regulation also defines the "operator" and "driver" of an autonomous vehicle as "the person [who] causes the autonomous vehicle to engage, regardless of whether the person is physically present in the vehicle while it is engaged."[533] This determination reduces, but does not eliminate, uncertainty regarding the application of rules of the road to the automated vehicle's user.[534]

In understanding the remaining portions of the regulation, it is important to distinguish between (1) the testing of autonomous vehicles for research and development and (2) the sale and consumer operation of these vehicles by state residents. Although both are addressed in the regulation, testing receives more detailed treatment. As the DMV explains in its informational statement, "[s]ince the autonomous technology will not be available to the public immediately, the Department will be implementing the certification of compliance facilities and vehicle registration program requirements directly after completing the testing phase of this project."[535]

The safety requirements specified by the regulation generally apply to both test vehicles and consumer vehicles.[536] Both must have a separate data recorder that "capture[s] ... sensor data for at least 30 seconds before a collision occurs" and stores that data "for 3 years after the date of the collision," have a "switch to engage and disengage the autonomous vehicle," "safely alert the operator to take control ... if a technology failure is detected," and "not adversely affect any other safety features ... subject to federal regulation."[537] In addition, a test vehicle must be "safe to operate."[538] A consumer vehicle must additionally be "capable of being operated in compliance with the applicable traffic laws," "indicate whether [it] may be operated with or without the physical presence of an operator," be able to "safely move out of traffic and come to a stop" as required, have a visual indicator that it is operating autonomously, and "allow[] the operator," should the physical presence of one be required, "to take control of the autonomous vehicle in multiple manners."[539]

A person that wishes to test a vehicle must obtain a one-year license by completing the appropriate DMV form (currently available online),[540] affirming that the vehicle meets the relevant safety requirements above, showing insurance coverage, proving that its vehicles "have been driven by the applicant for a combined minimum of not less than 10,000 miles in autonomous mode" and "in various conditions for a number of miles that demonstrates the safety of the ... vehicles in those conditions," demonstrating the technology for approval, proposing geographic locations and establishing the capability of its vehicles in those conditions, providing a surety bond or cash,[541] providing other information required by the DMV, and applying for special license plates.[542] The DMV may deny, suspend, revoke, or not renew a testing license.[543]

A testing licensee may only test its vehicles in the general areas and conditions for which it has received approval.[544] These currently include six geographic categories (interstate highways, state highways, urban environments, complex urban environments,[545] residential roads, and unpaved/unmarked roads) and five environmental types (night driving, rain, fog, snow/ice, and wind); more detail about these categories is provided in the application packet available online.[546] At least two trained persons who are licensed in their state of residence must be physically present in and actively monitoring the vehicle at all times during highway testing, unless this requirement is waived by the DMV.[547] In addition, the licensee must report all crashes and citations to the DMV.[548]

The remaining significant regulatory provisions apply only to consumer vehicles and not to test vehicles. Moreover, the provisions governing sale apply only to sales within the state,[549] and the provisions governing operation apply only to operation by residents of the state.[550]

A "certificate of compliance" is required "[b]efore an autonomous vehicle may be offered for sale by a licensed vehicle dealer" and "[b]efore an autonomous vehicle may be registered."[551] As noted, it is not required for testing.[552] It can be issued by a manufacturer of the autonomous vehicle or by a licensed "autonomous technology certification facility"—

though, as also noted below, the text is not entirely clear how this applies to the manufacturer.[553] The issuer certifies that the installed autonomous technology meets the relevant safety standards and that the owner's manual "describes any limitations and capabilities of the autonomous vehicle."[554]

An applicant to operate a certification facility must complete the appropriate DMV form (which is not yet available), "submit such proof as the [DMV] deems necessary or appropriate to demonstrate that the applicant possesses the necessary knowledge and expertise to certify the safety of autonomous vehicles including, without limitation, whether the autonomous vehicles meet the requirements for the issuance of a certificate of compliance," provide a surety bond or cash of $500,000, make its facility available for inspection and, if required, "demonstrate the manner in which autonomous vehicles will be certified," and make financial information available.[555] A successful applicant may then issue a certificate of compliance "to a manufacturer of an autonomous vehicle or to any other person who wishes to obtain such a certificate for a new or used vehicle with autonomous technology."[556] Notably, however, a manufacturer can also issue its own certificate.[557] The DMV may deny, suspend, or revoke a certification facility license.[558]

A person who holds a Nevada driver's license and "wishes to operate an autonomous vehicle in autonomous mode in [the] State" must obtain a "G" endorsement on her license.[559] Such an endorsement is not required for testing or for out-of-state drivers.[560] The applicant must complete the appropriate DMV form (which is not yet available), "acknowledge that the operator is subject at all times to the traffic laws and other laws," and "provide such additional information as the [DMV] deems necessary."[561]

To register an autonomous vehicle in Nevada, its owner must submit, inter alia, a copy of the certificate of compliance and proof of insurance coverage.[562] Upon registration, the DMV "will issue license plates to the owner of the vehicle indicating that the vehicle is an autonomous vehicle."[563]

6.4.2   Florida Recognizes the Legality of These Vehicles

With its enactment of Committee Substitute House Bill (CS/HB) 1207 in 2012, Florida became the second US state to expressly regulate autonomous driving.[564] The legislation:

- defines "autonomous vehicle" and "autonomous technology";[565]

- declares the legislature's intent to promote autonomous technology;[566]

- "finds that the state does not prohibit or specifically regulate the testing or operation of autonomous technology in motor vehicles on public roads";[567]

- states that a "person who possesses a valid driver license may operate an autonomous vehicle in autonomous mode";[568]

- deems the person who "causes the vehicle's autonomous technology to engage" to be the operator of that vehicle;[569]

- specifies certain requirements for autonomous vehicles registered in the state;[570]

- specifies certain requirements for testing an autonomous vehicle in the state;[571]

- recognizes limitations on the liability of "the original manufacturer" of a vehicle for "alleged defects" related to the conversion of that vehicle "by a third party into an autonomous vehicle";[572] and

- directs the preparation by February 12, 2014 of a report "recommending [any] additional legislative or regulatory action."

The entire legislation, which is less than three pages long, concisely details these provisions.

6.4.3   California Also Recognizes the Legality of These Vehicles

With its enactment of Senate Bill (SB) 1298 in 2012, California became the third US state to expressly regulate autonomous driving.[573] The legislation:

- declares the legislature's intent to both promote and ensure the safety of autonomous vehicles;[574]

- finds that the state "presently does not prohibit or specifically regulate the operation of autonomous vehicles";[575]

- directs the state Department of Motor Vehicles to adopt rules by the beginning of 2015;[576]

- maintains the current legal status until these rules are adopted;[577]

- defines "autonomous vehicle" and "autonomous technology";[578]

- defines the operator as "the person who is seated in the driver's seat, or if there is no person in the driver's seat, causes the autonomous technology to engage";[579]

- specifies certain basic requirements for testing an autonomous vehicle;[580]

- specifies certain basic requirements for operating an autonomous vehicle;[581]

- specifies additional procedural steps to gain approval to operate an autonomous vehicle without a driver inside;[582] and

- requires manufacturers of autonomous technologies to disclose data collection to purchasers.[583]

6.4.4   Bills Have Been Introduced in Other States

For the current status of legislative efforts in other states (including Arizona, Hawaii, New Jersey, Oklahoma, and the District of Columbia), see the website cited below.[584]

6.5   States May Wish to Clarify the Legal Status of Automated Driving

The draft bill language that follows begins to address some of the issues raised in this paper. However, a bill that simply adopts this language would be incomplete and possibly premature. The language does not directly address vehicle standards, general tort liability, insurance, data collection, transportation planning, environmental impact assessment, or other areas relevant to automated vehicles. In addition, it is subject to revision; a current version is available at the website provided.[585]

The main feature of this draft is its distinction between an automated vehicle's ordinary and "virtual" drivers.[586] The natural person occupying or otherwise using an automated vehicle is subject to existing rules of the road unless the manufacturer or insurer of the vehicle has assumed these responsibilities by registering as a virtual driver. Explanation of the other provisions is provided in the accompanying footnotes.

1.   **Background.**

1.1.   Legislative intent. It is the intent of the Legislature to facilitate the development and deployment of automated vehicles in a way that improves highway safety.[587]

1.2.   Conventional operation. Nothing in this Act is intended or shall be construed to change existing statutory law as applied to vehicles neither under nor transitioning from automated operation.[588]

1.3.   Vehicle owners. Nothing in this Act is intended or shall be construed to abridge the existing statutory civil liability of any vehicle owner.[589]

1.4.   Geneva Convention. The Legislature hereby finds that automated operation of vehicles under the conditions prescribed herein is consistent with article 8 of the Convention on Road Traffic because (1) such operation has the potential to significantly improve highway safety, one of the objects of the Convention; (2) this State shall make such operation reasonably knowable to the foreign visitors contemplated by the Convention; (3) the Convention implicitly permits indirect control over vehicles and animals; (4) there shall remain a licensed driver of each vehicle who shall be able to specify or accept the parameters of operation; and (5) these parameters shall be consistent with the traffic laws of this State.[590]

2.   Agency implementation.

2.1.   The Department shall by rule define certain automation profiles.[591]

2.2.   The Department shall by rule define certain test vehicle profiles.[592]

2.3.   The Department shall by rule establish requirements for automation-only licenses.[593]

2.4.   The Department shall by rule establish requirements for virtual licenses.[594]

2.5.   The Department may by rule establish standards for the collection, transmission, retention, disclosure, use, or ownership of data generated by or for motor vehicles.[595]

2.6.   The Department shall make and maintain all other rules necessary to fully implement this Act, except that the Department may in its sole discretion decide to act through informal adjudication rather than through informal rulemaking.[596]

2.7.   The Department shall implement this Act in accordance with (1) all standards enacted by the National Highway Traffic Safety Administration and, to the extent that the Department in its sole discretion deems practicable, (2) relevant guidelines enacted by the National Highway Traffic Safety Administration, (3) relevant standards adopted by SAE International or the International Organization for Standardization, and (4) relevant regulations adopted by the Department of Motor Vehicles of the State of California.[597]

2.8.   The Department shall implement this Act in consultation with [the State Highway Patrol] and [the Department of Transportation], but the failure to consult shall not provide a basis for judicial invalidation of an otherwise lawful rule or decision.[598]

2.9.   The Department may recommend additional statutory changes to the Legislature.[599]

3.   **Definitions.**

3.1.   Automated operation means computer direction of a vehicle's steering, braking, and accelerating without real-time human input.[600]

3.2.   Automated vehicle means a motor vehicle capable of automated operation.[601]

3.3.   Automation package means the combination of hardware and software necessary for automated operation.[602]

3.4.   Automation period means the moment that automated operation begins until the moment that a natural person (1) provides real-time input other than to mitigate an imminent risk, (2) turns off the vehicle, or (3) otherwise acts as specified by rule of the Department.[603]

3.5.   Automation profile means a set of technical characteristics describing a particular kind of automated operation.[604]

3.6.   Department means the [Department of Motor Vehicles].[605]

3.7.   Drive and operate each mean [as provided in the vehicle code and case law], except that the effective driver exclusively drives and operates an automated vehicle during an automation period.[606]

3.8.   Driver and operator each mean [as provided in the vehicle code and case law], except that the effective driver is the exclusive driver and operator of an automated vehicle during an automation period.[607]

3.9.   Effective driver means:

3.9.1.   If automated operation is initiated to mitigate an imminent risk, the natural person operating the vehicle immediately prior to such initiation;[608]

3.9.2.   Else the vehicle's virtual driver;[609]

3.9.3.   Else the natural person who actually or, by rule of the Department, presumptively initiates automated operation;[610]

3.9.4.   Else the vehicle's owner;[611]

3.9.5.   Additionally any person who in willful or wanton disregard for the safety of persons or property activates, permits, or tampers with automated operation.[612]

3.10. Manufacturer means any person engaged in the business of constructing or assembling vehicles of a type required to be registered under [this title].[613]

3.11. Test vehicle means a vehicle registered as a platform for research, development, or demonstration of automated operation or, by rule of the Department, other safety-critical vehicle systems.[614]

3.12. Test vehicle profile means a set of technical characteristics describing a particular kind of test vehicle operation.[615]

3.13. Virtual driver means, with respect to an automated vehicle, any person holding a virtual license covering that vehicle for the pertinent part of its automation profile.[616]

4.   Vehicle registration.

4.1. When registering or renewing the registration of any motor vehicle, the Department shall ascertain and record that vehicle's (1) automation profile and (2) virtual driver, if any.[617]

4.2. Any modification to a motor vehicle or its equipment that alters its automation package shall invalidate its registration, unless such alteration is (1) required by law, (2) by or on behalf of the vehicle's manufacturer, (3) to a test vehicle in accordance with its registration, or (4) otherwise permitted by rule of the Department.[618]

4.3. The Department may decline to register or, with reasonable notice to the owner and the virtual license holder, suspend, revoke, or decline to renew the registration of any motor vehicle that it determines to be unsafe, improperly equipped, or otherwise unfit to be operated on a highway.[619]

4.4.   In making a determination regarding the registration of any motor vehicle, the Department may by rule or practice treat as conclusive a decision by the responsible agency of another state to permit or restrict the registration, sale, operation, or testing of the relevant make, model, kind, or category of motor vehicle or equipment.[620]

4.5.   The registration of a motor vehicle shall create no presumption as to the safety of that vehicle or its equipment.[621]

5.   Driver licensing.

5.1.   Automation-only license.[622]

5.1.1.   Any natural person of legal driving age who solely by reason of physical disability is ineligible for a [regular noncommercial] driving license shall be eligible for an automation-only license.

5.1.2.   Each automation-only license shall specify conditions of operation, including particular automation profiles to which it is restricted.

5.1.3.   Any person who holds a valid automation-only license may operate an automated vehicle in accordance with those conditions of operation.

5.2.   Virtual license.[623]

5.2.1.   Any person, natural or otherwise, who meets requirements established by the Department shall be eligible for a virtual license.[624]

5.2.2. Each virtual license shall cover a specific kind of automated vehicle for all or part of its automation profile.[625]

5.2.3. The Department may require that the holder of a virtual license be the manufacturer or insurer of the vehicles covered by that license.[626]

5.2.4. Any statutory requirements for a driving license that in the Department's determination reasonably pertain only to a natural person shall not apply to an applicant for a virtual license who is not a natural person.[627]

5.2.5. The Department may, with reasonable notice to the license holder and owner of any covered vehicle, suspend, revoke, or restrict a virtual license.[628]

6. Equipment.

6.1. General. [This title's] vehicle and equipment provisions shall be interpreted to facilitate the development and deployment of automated vehicles in a way that improves highway safety.[629]

6.2. Standards. Any vehicle sold, registered, modified for sale, or operated on any highway in this State shall comply with (1) all applicable standards enacted by the National Highway Traffic Safety Administration and (2) all applicable standards enacted by the Department.[630]

6.3. [Automated vehicles.][631]

7. Rules of the road.

7.1. General. [This title's] rules of the road shall be interpreted to facilitate the development and deployment of automated vehicles in a way that improves highway safety.[632]

7.2.   Qualitative standards. No rule shall be interpreted to impose a greater obligation on drivers of automated vehicles than on drivers of vehicles that are not automated, unless the Department by rule specifies otherwise.[633]

7.3.   Virtual drivers. Any language in [this title] that [the Department] by rule determines cannot reasonably refer to a virtual driver shall instead refer to a different person or to no person at all, in each case as specified in such rule.[634]

7.4.   Unattended vehicles. A vehicle that is under automated operation by a virtual driver shall not be deemed unattended unless it is not lawfully registered, poses a risk to public safety, or unreasonably obstructs other road users.[635]

7.5.   Abandoned vehicles. A vehicle that is under automated operation by a virtual driver shall not be deemed abandoned unless it is not lawfully registered, poses a risk to public safety, or unreasonably obstructs other road users.[636]

7.6.   Following distance. A platoon that consists of at least one vehicle under automated operation by a virtual driver and that is otherwise lawful and operating lawfully shall not be deemed in violation of following-distance requirements.[637]

7.7.   Reckless driving. Any person who in willful or wanton disregard for the safety of persons or property initiates, permits, or tampers with automated operation of a vehicle is guilty of reckless driving.[638]

7.8.   Unsafe vehicles. No person shall operate any vehicle that is unsafe, improperly equipped, or otherwise unfit to be operated.[639]

7.9.   Vehicular felonies. No person shall be guilty of any felony specified in [this title] without a culpability at least equal to that specified or, if none is specified, [gross negligence].[640]

7.10. Vehicular misdemeanors. No person shall be guilty of any misdemeanor specified in [this title] without a culpability at least equal to that specified or, if none is specified, [negligence].[641]

7.11. Due care in vehicles under automated operation. Notwithstanding other provisions of [this title] or of any local ordinance, every driver or occupant of a vehicle under automated operation shall exercise due care as circumstances require to avoid injury to any natural person.[642]

The foregoing draft language might provide at most a starting point for any jurisdiction's analysis. Consistency among states—and coordination with the federal government—may be highly desirable. At the same time, as this paper has documented, state vehicle codes vary in both form and substance. A legislature may want or need to delegate more or less discretionary authority to its department of motor vehicles or other responsible agency. And new technologies or business cases may require or merit revision of certain provisions—or even the entire approach. For these reasons and others, a current version of this language is available at the website provided.[643] The law of automated vehicles is necessarily living.

7   Conclusion

Current law probably does not prohibit automated vehicles—but may nonetheless discourage their introduction or complicate their operation. Key issues include the precise definition of these human-machine systems, the concept of control under the Geneva Convention, the potential for future regulation by the National Highway Traffic Safety Administration, and the application of myriad state laws concerning drivers and driving behavior. Five near-term recommendations might provide some initial clarity without placing law too far ahead of technology.

First, regulators and standards organizations should work to develop common vocabularies and definitions that are meaningful in both law and engineering and accessible to the public and the media.

Second, the United States should closely monitor efforts to amend or interpret the Vienna Convention as an example for or caution regarding any potential effort to clarify the Geneva Convention.

Third, NHTSA should provide public guidance about the likely scope and schedule of any initial regulatory action it may take with respect to automated vehicles.

Fourth, states should closely examine their vehicle codes to determine how those codes would or should apply to automated vehicles both with and without an identifiable human operator.

Finally, there may be value in further research on the regulatory regimes applicable to special motor vehicles, including taxicabs, trucks, buses, personal transporters (including Segways), golf carts, and low-speed vehicles. These technologies are important as potential applications for automated vehicles, and these regimes are important as potential analogies for the specific regulation of such vehicles.

More generally, the law plays a crucial role in creating, defining, discussing, and managing many of the risks and opportunities posed by automated vehicles. Clearly understanding the current legal status of these vehicles is therefore an important step toward ultimately realizing their potential.

8   Appendix 1: Many State Vehicle Codes Probably Do Prohibit Automated Vehicle Platoons

Vehicle platoons—convoys of tightly spaced and closely coordinated vehicles that use at least some automation[644]—are probably consistent with the Geneva Convention and federal motor vehicle safety standards but probably conflict with following-distance requirements in many US states.

The Geneva Convention recognizes that road traffic might move in groups. If platoons are treated as convoys, the Convention imposes no hard requirements beyond compliance with domestic law: "Convoys of vehicles and animals shall have the number of drivers prescribed by domestic regulations" and "shall, if necessary, be divided into sections of moderate length, and be sufficiently spaced out for the convenience of traffic."[645]

Platoons likewise do not appear to be uniquely burdened by any federal motor vehicle safety standard, subject to the same caveats noted above.[646] Federal rules specific to commercial operations, including trucks, trucking, and truckers, may be particularly relevant to platoons but are outside this paper's scope.

Platoons implicate many of the state laws discussed above[647] and raise at least three additional issues.[648] The first is straightforward: Each platoon is likely to be treated as a series of vehicles rather than as a single vehicle. A "[v]ehicle" is generally "[e]very device in, upon, or by which any person or property is or may be transported or drawn upon a highway, excepting devices used exclusively upon stationary rails or tracks,"[649] and even truck tractors, trailers, and semitrailers are typically treated as separate vehicles.[650]

The second issue involves the identity of each vehicle's driver. Some states define driver to expressly include a person "who is exercising control of a vehicle or steering a vehicle being towed by a motor vehicle,"[651] but this is not a uniform conclusion.[652] Given the expansive way in which driver and related terms are defined and interpreted,[653] the primary occupants of the lead vehicle and the following vehicles might each qualify as drivers of all or some of the platoon vehicles.[654]

The third issue is vehicle spacing. Research platoons have featured vehicle gaps as low as three to four meters (10 to 13 feet) to improve fuel efficiency and to limit incursions by other vehicles.[655] However, nearly every jurisdiction prohibits drivers from following too closely,[656] and violation of this restriction can constitute negligence per se.[657]

In particular, most states impose some variation of the requirement that "[t]he driver of a vehicle shall not follow another vehicle more closely than is reasonable and prudent, having due regard for the speed of such vehicles and the traffic upon and the condition of the highway."[658] The effect of this general rule depends entirely on the interpretation of qualitative terms like "reasonable and prudent."[659]

Most states also require certain drivers who are outside business and residential districts to leave enough space that another vehicle may "enter and occupy such space without danger."[660] This restriction typically applies to trucks and to motor vehicles with trailers;[661] some states exclude truck lanes,[662] and some define a specific minimum distance between 150 feet and 500 feet.[663] Many states also apply this general restriction to motor vehicles "in a caravan or motorcade" other than a funeral procession,[664] with a smaller number defining a specific minimum distance between 100 and 300 feet.[665]

Unlike many of the other state law provisions discussed, the intent rather than merely the wording of many of these provisions is in conflict with platoon operations: Caravans may not exclude other vehicles. However, unlike many of the issues discussed, this restriction could be addressed with a fairly straightforward statutory change: A legislature might choose to exempt certain vehicles operating on certain facilities subject to certain conditions.[666]

9   Notes

[1] *United States v. Gourde*, 440 F.3d 1065, 1081 (9th Cir. 2006). *But see infra* note 8.

[2] *See id.* (citing *Kordel v. United States*, 335 U.S. 345, 348-49, 69 S.Ct. 106, 93 L.Ed. 52 (1948)); *see also, e.g., United States v. Davis*, 576 F.2d 1065, 1069 (3d Cir. 1978) ("Although proper judicial interpretation of any federal statute is always important, proper judicial interpretation of a criminal statute is critical. The maxim *nullum crimen sine lege, nulla poena sine lege* [no crime without law, no punishment without law] reminds us that the courts may not punish conduct as criminal unless that conduct has transgressed the clear, plain, or fair meaning of the defined offense."); *Hirota v. Gen. of the Army Douglas MacArthur*, 338 U.S. 197, 69 S. Ct. 1238, 93 L. Ed. 1902 (1949) (Douglas, J., concurring); *infra* note 199.

[3] *See, e.g.*, Richard H. Steinberg, *Who Is Sovereign?*, 40 Stan. J. Int'l L. 329, 345 n.13 (2004) ("[I]t is well established that state behavior that is not prohibited is permitted under international law.") (citing *Legality of the Threat or Use of Nuclear Weapons*, 1996 I.C.J. 226 (July 8, 1996)); Sir John Laws, *Beyond Rights*, 23 Oxford J. Legal Stud. 265, 273 (2003) ("The first—I have a right to do something if I have no obligation not to do it—reflects the general principle of the common law, that for the individual citizen, everything that is not forbidden is allowed."); Donna E. Arzt, *Soviet Anti-Semitism: Legal Responses in an Age of Glasnost*, 4 Temp. Int'l & Comp. L.J. 163, 166 (1990) ("There is only one basic principle; information that discloses state secrets or is capable of damaging the country's interests is prohibited. There is also only one formula for everything else: Anything that is not prohibited is permitted.") (quoting former media censor); *Queensborough Land Co. v. Cazeaux*, 136 La. 724, 734 (La. 1915) ("[A] general principle" in French property law is that "whatever is not prohibited is permitted.") (quoting Toullier); Stephen J. Werber, *Cloning: A Jewish Law Perspective with A Comparative Study of Other Abrahamic Traditions*, 30 Seton Hall L. Rev. 1114, 1135 (2000) ("[A] basic precept of Jewish law is that that which is not prohibited is permitted.").

[4] *See* Otis R. Damslet, *Same-Sex Marriage*, 10 N.Y.L. Sch. J. Hum. Rts. 555, 566 n.46 (1993) (quoting *On the Record*, Time, Mar. 18, 1985, at 73 ("In Germany, under the law everything is prohibited except that which is permitted. In France, under the law everything is permitted except that which is prohibited. In the Soviet Union, everything is prohibited, including that which is permitted. And in

Italy, under the law everything is permitted, especially that which is prohibited.") and Don Wallace, Jr., *Address to the 33rd Annual Meeting of the Section of Antitrust Law of the America Bar Association*, 54 Antitrust L.J. 571, 571 (1985) ("There was a column written—and he actually did this—in the Washington Post by Lloyd Cutler while he was counsel to President Carter. He was trying to distinguish between the Anglo American, German, and French approach to the law. He said of the common law approach, that anything was allowed unless it were prohibited by law; the German approach was that everything is prohibited unless permitted by law; and the French approach is that everything is prohibited but anything can be arranged.")); Richard A. Epstein, *The Permit Power Meets the Constitution*, 81 Iowa L. Rev. 407, 407-08 (1995) ("An old observation of the German system of freedom is that all which is not permitted is prohibited (which is at least better than what I take sometimes to be the modern American position that all which is not prohibited is required)."). *But see* Grundgesetz [German Basic Law] art. 2 par. 1 ("Jeder hat das Recht auf die freie Entfaltung seiner Persönlichkeit, soweit er nicht die Rechte anderer verletzt und nicht gegen die verfassungsmäßige Ordnung oder das Sittengesetz verstößt.") ["Every person shall have the right to free development of his personality insofar as he does not violate the rights of others or offend against the constitutional order or the moral law."]; *see also, e.g., Elfes Urteil*, BVerfGE 6, 32, 1 BvR 253/56 (Bundesverfassungsgericht [Federal Constitutional Court] Jan. 16, 1957) (broadly construing article 2, concluding that the right to travel abroad flows from it, and preventing Wilhelm Elfes from exercising that right); *Reiten im Walde*, BVerfGE 80, 137, 1 BvR 921/85 (Bundesverfassungsgericht June 6, 1989) (endorsing the broad construction of article 2 and concluding that specific restrictions on riding horses in the woods are consistent with that construction).

[5] *See, e.g.,* Tyler Cowen, *Can I See Your License, Registration and C.P.U.*, N.Y. Times, May 28, 2011 ("The driverless car is illegal in all 50 states."); Florida House of Representatives, Final Bill Analysis, CS/HB   1207,   Summary   Analysis, www.myfloridahouse.gov/Sections/Documents/loaddoc.aspx?FileNa me=h1207z1.THSS.DOCX&DocumentType=Analysis&BillNumber=1 207&Session=2012, at 2 ("The only jurisdiction in the world where it is legal to operate autonomous vehicles on public roads is in the state of Nevada, where a law authorizing them passed in June 2011."); *Autonomous   car,*   Wikipedia, en.wikipedia.org/wiki/Autonomous_car (October 1, 2012) ("One of the most significant obstacles to the proliferation of autonomous cars is the fact that they are illegal on most public roads.").

[6] *See generally, e.g.*, Stephen N. Roberts, Alison S. Hightower, Michael G. Thornton, Linda N. Cunningham, and Richard G. Terry, *Advanced Vehicle Control Systems: Potential Tort Liability for Developers*, FHWA Contract DTFH61-93-C-00087 (Dec. 1, 1993); Nidhi Kalra, James Anderson, Martin Wachs (RAND Corporation), *Liability and Regulation of Autonomous Vehicle Technologies*, California PATH Research Report, UCB-ITS-PRR-2009-28, 6-8 (April 2009).

[7] *See, e.g.*, Cal. Evid. Code § 669; Cal. Civ. Prac. Torts § 25:26. Notably, "[t]his presumption may be rebutted by proof that ... [t]he person violating the statute, ordinance, or regulation did what might reasonably be expected of a person of ordinary prudence, acting under similar circumstances, who desired to comply with the law." Cal. Evid. Code § 669(b).

[8] *See, e.g.*, *Geier v. Am. Honda Motor Co.*, 529 U.S. 861 (2000) (holding as a matter of implied preemption that a federal motor vehicle safety standard that required airbags in only some new vehicles meant that the lack of an airbag could not constitute a defect for the purpose of state product liability law). In general, however, "it does not follow that merely because one has complied with the terms of a statute or ordinance that one is absolved from negligence." Cal. Civ. Prac. Torts § 25:26; *see also Cipollone v. Liggett Group, Inc.*, 593 F. Supp. 1146, 1170 (D.N.J. 1984) ("The arguments presented by the defendants in this case symbolize a common misperception of the function of government regulation and the imposition of standards of conduct which result. It would be inappropriate to conclude that what is not prohibited is permitted or that a minimum standard fixes the maximum as well. It is impossible for the government to codify every act which should not be done or the standards by which every act should be performed. Thus, government has frequently established standards in those areas in which a particular industry has failed to establish its own. But injuries to persons, property and the environment were wrong even before government declared that they were wrong. Now that government has acted in many areas and decreed safety and quality standards, it would be unfortunate if those directed to do no less, assume that they need do no more. In almost every instance, government standards are meant to fix a level of performance below which one should not fall. However, legal minimums were never intended to supplant moral maximums. Nor were they intended to eliminate pride in quality and craftsmanship or self-imposed standards of health and safety."), *rev'd*, 789 F.2d 181 (3d. Cir. 1986).

[9] *Cf., e.g.*, Bailey Kuklin and Jeffrey W. Stempel, Foundations of the law: an interdisciplinary and jurisprudential primer (1994). Even private standards can arguably behave like law. *Cf.* Gillian E. Metzger, *Privatization As Delegation*, 103 Colum. L. Rev. 1367 (2003).

[10] Statute of the International Court of Justice art. 38.

[11] National Committee on Uniform Traffic Laws and Ordinances (NCUTLO), Millennium Edition of the Uniform Vehicle Code (2000) [hereinafter Uniform Veh. Code]. The Uniform Vehicle Code has shaped or reflected the motor vehicle codes of many states since it was first published in 1924. *See infra* part 6. The most recent version was released in 2000 by the National Committee on Uniform Traffic Laws and Ordinances (NCUTLO), a private nonprofit organization that "suspended operations about five years ago due to lack of funding." March 20, 2012 email from NCUTLO's former executive director (on file with author).

[12] A platoon is a convoy of tightly spaced and closely coordinated vehicles that operates with at least some automation. *See* Tom Robinson and Eric Chan, *Operating Platoons on Public Motorways: An Introduction to the SARTRE Platooning Programme*, www.sartre-project.eu/en/publications/Documents/SARTRE_Overview_Final_Pa per_ITS_World_Congress_2010.pdf at 2. Notable research includes the Safe Road Trains for the Environment (SARTRE) project, *see About the SARTRE project*, www.sartre-project.eu/en/about/Sidor/default.aspx, and the earlier National Automated Highways System Consortium, *see* University of California PATH, *Fact Sheet, Vehicle Platooning and Automated Highways*, www.path.berkeley.edu/path/Publications/Media/FactSheet/VPlatoon ing.pdf.

[13] *See infra* part 8.

[14] *River Wear Comm'rs v. Adamson*, 2 AC 743 (1877) (Lord Blackburn); *see generally* Norman J. Singer and J.D. Shambie Singer, *Standards of judgment: intent of the legislature*, 2A Sutherland Statutory Construction § 45:5 (7th ed.) ("The question of meaning lies deeper than the law. It involves questions of judgment too subtle for articulation and issues of the transference of knowledge as yet not fully understood by lawyers, scientists or psychologists inter alia.").

[15] Despite a "trend" toward interpreting public-safety legislation liberally to advance its basic purpose of preventing physical harm, "courts have not developed a uniform attitude or policy in its

construction. In many cases, courts have expressed, or have seemed to follow, a strict interpretation." Norman J. Singer and J.D. Shambie Singer, *Statutes enacted for the public safety*, 3A Sutherland Statutory Construction § 73:4 (7th ed.).

[16] Cal. Veh. Code § 22350.

[17] Cal. Veh. Code § 670.

[18] *People v. Fong*, 21 Cal. Rptr. 2d 907 (Cal. App. 1993).

[19] Cal. Veh. Code § 21200.

[20] *Fong*, 21 Cal. Rptr. 2d at 908; *see also McBoyle v. United States.*, 283 U.S. 25, 51 S. Ct. 340, 75 L. Ed. 816 (1931) (Holmes, J.) (strictly interpreting a criminal statute to hold that an airplane is not a vehicle under the National Motor Vehicle Theft Act); ABC News, *Men Busted for Riding Horse Drunk* (January 12, 2011), abcnews.go.com/US/video/men-busted-for-riding-horse-drunk-12598140 (discussing whether a Texas statute criminalizing the intoxicated operation of a motor vehicle includes riding a horse).

[21] Vienna Convention on the Law of Treaties, May 23, 1969, 1155 U.N.T.S. 331, 8 I.L.M. 679 (1969), art. 31. The United States, like all states, is bound by customary international law—norms that are established through state belief and practice rather than through treaties. Some of these norms with respect to treaties have been codified in the 1969 Vienna Convention on the Law of Treaties (VCLT). Although the United States is not a party to the VCLT and this treaty does not apply retroactively to the Geneva Convention, those portions of the VCLT that codify customary law are useful as an expression of that binding law.

[22] *Id.* art. 31.

[23] *Id.* art. 33.

[24] *Id.* art. 32.

[25] *Judgment of 4 April 2000*, European Court of Human Rights App. no. 26629/95, *cited in* Richard K. Gardiner, Treaty Interpretation (2008), at 39; *see also, e.g.*, *Legality of the Threat or Use of Nuclear Weapons*, 1996 I.C.J. 226 (July 8, 1996), par. 86.

[26] This broad definition includes any vehicle that is autonomous under Nevada, Florida, or California law, *see infra* part 6.4, or that is partially, highly, or fully automated under the German classification, *see infra* note 34. Real-time input could be provided by nonhuman systems external to the vehicle. In this way, the definition includes connected vehicles, *see* Steven E. Shladover, *Cooperative (Rather*

than Autonomous) Vehicle-Highway Automation Systems, IEEE Intelligent Transportation Systems Magazine, Spring 2009, ieeexplore.ieee.org/stamp/stamp.jsp?tp=&arnumber=5117654&tag= 1, and conventional vehicles that are operated by a physically distinct robot, *cf.* US Defense Advanced Research Projects Agency (DARPA), *Broad Agency Announcement, DARPA Robotics Challenge*, Tactical Technology Office (TTO), DARPA-BAA-12-39 (April 10, 2012), www.fbo.gov/spg/ODA/DARPA/CMO/DARPA-BAA-12-39/listing.html ("For Event 1 (drive a utility vehicle to the site) the robot must demonstrate mounted mobility by ingress to the vehicle, driving it on a road, and egress from the vehicle. The robot must also demonstrate manipulation by operating the controls, including steering, throttle, brakes, and ignition."); *DARPA seeks robot enthusiasts (and you) to face off for $2M prize!*, April 10, 2012, www.darpa.mil/NewsEvents/Releases/2012/04/10.aspx. This paper does not examine laws specific to trucks, buses, and taxicabs.

[27] *See* Wuhong Wang, Fuguo Hou, Huachun Tan, and Heiner Bubb, *A Framework for Function Allocations in Intelligent Driver Interface Design for Comfort and Safety*, International Journal of Computational Intelligence Systems, vol. 3, no. 5, 531, 535-36 (2010); Dagmar Kern and Albrecht Schmidt, *Design Space for Driver-based Automotive User Interfaces*, Proceedings of the First International Conference on Automotive User Interfaces and Interactive Vehicular Applications (2009); Thomas A. Ranney, *Models of Driving Behavior: A Review of Their Evolution*, Accident Analysis and Prevention, vol. 26, no. 6, 733, 741-43 (1994); Pravin Varaiya and Steven E. Shladover, *Sketch of an IVHS Systems Architecture* (1990, rev. 1991) (discussing route, path, and maneuver); Kalra, *supra* note 6, at 6-8 (2009) (discussing sensing, planning and acting).

[28] *See supra* note 27.

[29] *Id.*

[30] *Id.*

[31] Consider, for example, antilock brakes, electronic stability control, and conventional as well as adaptive cruise control.

[32] *Cf.* Shladover, *supra* note 26 (discussing cooperative systems).

[33] Domain in this sense includes traffic complexity (ranging from facilities used only by vehicles of a certain type to urban streets used by a variety of motor vehicle, bicycle, and pedestrian traffic), environmental conditions (ranging from dry to snowy and from dark to sunny), and vehicle speed (ranging from the very low speeds

characteristic of parking maneuvers to the high speeds characteristic of freeways).

[34] Tom M. Gasser (Projektgruppenleitung), Clemens Arzt, Mihiar Ayoubi, Arne Bartels, Lutz Bürkle, Jana Eier, Frank Flemisch, Dirk Häcker, Tobias Hesse, Werner Huber, Christine Lotz, Markus Maurer, Simone Ruth-Schumacher, Jürgen Schwarz, und Wolfgang Vogt, *Rechstfolgen zunehmender Fahrzeugautomatisierung, Gemeinsamer Schlussbericht der Projektgruppe*, Berichte der Bundesanstalt für Straßenwesen (BASt), Fahrzeugtechnik Heft F 83 (2012) at 9. This report on the "legal consequences of increasing vehicle automation" is impressive. To order it as a German-language hardcopy on BASt's website, see *Rechtsfolgen zunehmender Fahrzeugautomatisierung*, www.bast.de/nn_42254/DE/Publikationen/Berichte/unterreihe-f/2013-2012/f83.html.

[35] *See generally infra* part 6.4 (describing autonomous driving laws in Nevada, Florida, and California).

[36] The BASt report, for example, defines five levels of automation: driver only, assisted, partially automated, highly automated, and fully automated. Gasser, *supra* note 34, at 9 (defining five levels of automation:); *see also* HAVEit, Highly automated vehicles for intelligent transport, 7th Framework programme, ICT-2007.6.1, *The future of driving, Deliverable D61.1, Final Report*, haveit-eu.org/LH2Uploads/ItemsContent/24/HAVEit_212154_D61.1_Final_Report_Published.pdf, 28 (describing automation as a spectrum ranging from complete human control to complete computer control); Thomas B. Sheridan, Telerobotics, Automation, and Human Supervisory Control (1992), 260 (defining multiple levels).

[37] The BASt report identifies maximum operating speed as a second dimension, which divides into low speeds (parking and shunting), medium speeds (traffic jams and city driving), and high speeds (motorways). Gasser, *supra* note 34, at 9. The leader of the project group subsequently suggested a potential third dimension, namely the length of time that a particular function is used. *See* Tom M. Gasser and Daniel Westhoff, *BASt-study: Definitions of Automation and Legal Issues in Germany*, 2012 Road Vehicle Automation Workshop, Transportation Research Board, July 25, 2012, onlinepubs.trb.org/onlinepubs/conferences/2012/Automation/present ations/Gasser.pdf at 6. Steven E. Shladover offers a useful taxonomy of driving environments. Steven E. Shladover, *Automated Vehicles: Terminology and Taxonomy*, 2012 Road Vehicle Automation Workshop, Transportation Research Board, July 25, 2012,

onlinepubs.trb.org/onlinepubs/conferences/2012/Automation/present ations/Shladover1.pdf. And a federal working group sponsored by the National Institute for Standards and Technology (NIST) describes "contextual autonomy" in three dimensions: the complexity of the mission assigned to the system, the complexity of the environment in which that system performs its mission, and the degree to which that performance is performed without human involvement. Hui-Min Huang, *Autonomy Levels for Unmanned Systems (ALFUS) Framework: Safety and Application Issues*, www.nist.gov/customcf/get_pdf.cfm?pub_id=823619.

[38] The National Highway Traffic Safety Administration (NHTSA) and SAE International's On-Road Autonomous Vehicle Standards Committee (on which I serve) have yet to finalize their approaches. *See* John Maddox, Associate Administrator, Vehicle Safety Research, NHTSA, Keynote Address to Association of Unmanned Vehicle Systems International (AUVSI)'s Driverless Car Summit, June 13, 2012 at 14 (draft definitions); SAE International On-Road Autonomous Vehicle Standards Committee, www.sae.org/works/committeeHome.do?comtID=TEVAVS. The International Organization for Standardization (ISO) has published standards for adaptive cruise control (ACC), traffic impediment warning systems, and functional safety and is now developing a lanekeeping standard, but it has not placed these systems within a larger taxonomy of automation. *See* ISO 15622:2010, *Intelligent transport systems – Adaptive Cruise Control systems – Performance requirements and test procedures*, www.iso.org/iso/iso_catalogue/catalogue_tc/catalogue_detail.htm?cs number=50024; ISO/TS 15624:2001, *Transport information and control systems – Traffic Impediment Warning Systems (TIWS) – System requirements*, www.iso.org/iso/iso_catalogue/catalogue_tc/catalogue_detail.htm?cs number=27833; ISO 26262:2011, *Road vehicles – Functional safety*, www.iso.org/iso/catalogue_detail?csnumber=43464 (nine parts total); ISO/CD 11270, *Intelligent transport systems – Lane keeping assist systems (LKAS)*, www.iso.org/iso/iso_catalogue/catalogue_tc/catalogue_detail.htm?cs number=50347.

[39] *See* Defense Science Board, *The Role of Autonomy in DoD Systems*, July 2012, www.fas.org/irp/agency/dod/dsb/autonomy.pdf at 23-24 ("The pervasive effort to define autonomy and to create vehicle autonomy roadmaps is counterproductive.... The attempt to define autonomy has resulted in a waste of both time and money spent debating and reconciling different terms and may be contributing to fears of unbounded autonomy.... A negative

consequence of the commitment to levels of autonomy is that it deflects focus from the fact that all autonomous systems are joint human-machine cognitive systems, thus resulting in brittle designs.").

[40] Although both "automation" and "autonomy" are frequently used to mean computer control, these words have subtly different meanings. *Compare Automation*, Oxford English Dictionary ("The action or process of introducing automatic equipment or devices into a manufacturing or other process or facility; (also) the fact of making something (as a system, device, etc.) automatic.") (selected definition) *with Autonomy*, Oxford English Dictionary ("With reference to a thing: the fact or quality of being unrelated to anything else, self-containedness; independence from external influence or control, self-sufficiency.") (selected definition). Automation describes the replacement of human labor through technology; "automated driving" is therefore driving performed by a computer. In contrast, autonomy describes a system's independence from external control; "autonomous driving" is therefore driving performed by itself. Without careful identification of the system and its boundaries, this term is unclear. Steven E. Shladover argues that the use of the term "autonomous" in this sense is incorrect rather than merely unclear. *See* Shladover (2009), *supra* note 26. The level of autonomy (or, conversely, cooperation) refers to the degree to which driver-vehicle pairs are isolated from each other. *Id.* Under this conception, today's vehicles are largely autonomous. *Id.* In contrast, vehicles that are tightly coordinated with each other (through vehicle-to-vehicle communication known as "V2V") and with infrastructure (through vehicle-to-infrastructure communication known as "V2I") would be both automated and cooperative but not autonomous. *Id.* Yet another conception of these terms treats "autonomous driving" as "[t]he extreme end result of automated driving." Margriet van Schijndel-de Nooij, Bastiaan Krosse, Thijs van den Broek, Sander Maas, Ellen van Nunen, Han Zwijnenberg, Anna Schieben, Henning Mosebach, Nick Ford, Mike McDonald, David Jeffery, Jinan Piao, and Javier Sanchez, *Definition of necessary vehicle and infrastructure systems for Automated Driving*, SMART 2010/0064, Study Report v 1.2 for European Commission (2011), ec.europa.eu/information_society/activities/esafety/doc/studies/auto mated/reportfinal.pdf, at 12. Under this conception, automated driving overlaps with cooperative driving, which includes both "automotive and road traffic systems." *Id.* at 11. Statutes in Nevada, Florida, and California reference "autonomous vehicles," *see infra* part 6.4, as do many media articles, *see autonomous driving v. self-driving v. driverless*, Google Insights for Search, www.google.com/insights/search/#q=autonomous%20driving%2Csel

f-driving%2Cdriverless&gprop=news. Ultimately, the technical, legal, and popular usages of these terms may or may not coalesce.

[41] This assumption is critical to the conclusions that follow. The conclusion that "automated vehicles are legal" is limited in the same way that the assertion about the legality of any product (including motor vehicles) is limited: They must all meet certain standards, which in the case of motor vehicles includes some level of safe performance. *See infra* parts 5, 6.3.

[42] Similarly, technical control, technical responsibility, legal control, and legal responsibility are probably not coextensive concepts. In the legal context, this raises questions regarding vicarious and other forms of strict liability, culpability (mens rea), and conduct by actors subject to the law (actus reus).

[43] *See infra* part 6.2.2.

[44] Automation could also *increase* standardization and aggregation. *See, e.g.*, Lisa Shay, Woodrow Hartzog, John Nelson, Dominic Larkin, and Gregory Conti, *Confronting Automated Law Enforcement*, robots.law.miami.edu/wp-content/uploads/2012/01/Shay-EtAl-ConfrontingAutomatedLawEnf.pdf, at 19; *infra* part 4.4.

[45] The legal response to these developments has not been entirely satisfactory. *See, e.g.*, Ralph D. Clifford, *Intellectual Property in the Era of the Creative Computer Program: Will the True Creator Please Stand Up?*, 71 Tul. L. Rev. 1675, 1696-97 (1997) (noting an implicit requirement in patent law that the inventor be human); *Citizens United v. Fed. Election Comm'n*, 130 S. Ct. 876, 175 L. Ed. 2d 753 (2010) (overturning campaign spending restrictions on corporations and unions as a violation of the first amendment's protection of free speech).

[46] *See infra* part 4.1.

[47] *See infra* part 4.2.

[48] *See infra* parts 4.3-4.4.

[49] *See infra* part 4.5.

[50] Convention on Road Traffic, Geneva, September 19, 1949, 125 U.N.T.S. 3, 3 U.S.T. 3008, T.I.A.S. No. 2487, treaties.un.org/pages/ViewDetailsV.aspx?&src=TREATY&mtdsg_no=XI~B~1&chapter=11&Temp=mtdsg5&lang=en [hereinafter Geneva Convention].

[51] *See id.* art. 24 ("Each Contracting State shall allow any driver admitted to its territory who fulfils [certain] conditions ... and who holds a valid driving permit issued to him ... to drive [certain motor vehicles] on its roads without further examination.... A Contracting State may however require that any driver admitted to its territory shall carry an international driving permit conforming to the model....").

[52] *Id.* at pmbl.

[53] United Nations Economic and Social Council, United Nations Conference on Road and Motor Transport, Committee II on Technical Conditions to be Fulfilled by Vehicles, *Summary Record of the Seventeenth Meeting, Held at the Palais des Nations, Geneva, on Tuesday, 6 September 1949 at 9.45 a.m.*, E/CONF.8/C.II/SR.17 Rev. 1 (18 November 1949) at 7 [Scan 18506]. This paper usually references the revised version ("Rev.") of the Geneva conference's summary records when the pertinent pages of that version are available and legible.

[54] *See* Geneva Convention, *supra* note 50, arts. 7 ("Every driver, pedestrian or other road user shall conduct himself in such a way as not to endanger or obstruct traffic; he shall avoid all behaviour that might cause damage to persons, or public or private property."), 8 ("5. Drivers shall at all times be able to control their vehicles or guide their animals. When approaching other road users, they shall take such precautions as may be required for the safety of the latter."), 9 ("As a general rule and whenever the provisions of Article 7 so require, every driver shall: (a) on two-lane carriageways intended for two-way traffic, keep his vehicle in the lane appropriate to the direction in which he is travelling; (b) on carriageways with more than two lanes, keep his vehicle in the lane nearest to the edge of the carriageway appropriate to the direction in which he is travelling."), 10 ("The driver of a vehicle shall at all times have its speed under control and shall drive in a reasonable and prudent manner. He shall slow down or stop whenever circumstances so require, and particularly when visibility is not good."), 12 ("1. Every driver approaching a fork, crossroads, road junction or level-crossing shall take special precautions to avoid accidents...."), 13 ("Drivers shall not leave vehicles or animals until they have taken all necessary precautions to avoid an accident."). In addition to these obligations, a driver arguably has rights as well. *See* art. 24 ("Each Contracting State shall allow any driver admitted to its territory [who has met certain conditions] ... to drive on its roads without further examination [certain] motor vehicles....").

[55] Geneva Convention, *supra* note 50, art. 8 (emphasis added).

[56] *Id.* art. 4.

[57] *Id.* art. 4.

[58] Geneva Convention, *supra* note 50, art. 30; *see* International Convention relating to Road Traffic, Paris, April 24, 1926, 1929 L.N.T.S. 82, No. 2220 [hereinafter 1926 Road Traffic Convention]; International Convention relative to Motor Traffic, Paris, April 24, 1926, 1930 L.N.T.S. 123, No. 2505 [hereinafter 1926 Motor Traffic Convention]; Convention on the Regulation of Inter-American Automotive Traffic, Washington, December 15, 1943, www.oas.org/dil/treaties_C-11_Convention_on_the_Regulation_of_Inter-American_Auto-Motive_Traffic.PDF [hereinafter 1943 Convention]. Only the French texts of the two 1926 treaties are authoritative. *See* 1926 Road Traffic Convention at 1; 1926 Motor Traffic Convention at 1. It is conceivable that they still govern relations between certain states.

[59] 1926 Motor Traffic Convention at pmbl.; *see* Convention with respect to the International Circulation of Motor Vehicles, signed at Paris, October 11, 1909, 4 Am. J. Intl. L. 316, 316-328 (1910), www.jstor.org/stable/2212082 [hereinafter 1909 Convention]. This paper uses the term "treaty" to refer to each negotiated document, but other uses are possible. *See* Vienna Convention on the Law of Treaties, *supra* note 21, art. 2(2).

[60] This treaty continues to govern relations between the United States and nine states (Brazil, Colombia, Costa Rica, El Salvador, Honduras, Mexico, Nicaragua, Panama, and Uruguay) that have not ratified the Geneva Convention. Organization of American States, *Signatories and Ratifications, Convention on the Regulation of Inter-American Auto-Motive Traffic*, www.oas.org/dil/treaties_C-11_Convention_on_the_Regulation_of_Inter-American_Auto-Motive_Traffic_sign.htm.

[61] As the lead US representative to the Geneva conference explained, "The United States had been represented at the 1926 Conference merely by a delegation of six observers. It had therefore been unable to accede to or ratify the Conventions which that Conference had drawn up.... [H]is country now realised the importance and necessity of a world-wide convention in the field of road transport." United Nations Economic and Social Council, United Nations Conference on Road and Motor Transport, *Summary Record of the Second Meeting, Held at the Palais des Nations, Geneva, on Wednesday, 24 August 1949 at 10 a.m.,* E/CONF.8/SR.2.Rev.1 (14 November 1949) at 10 [Scan 18588]. Indeed, US motorists in 1949 "operate[d] a total of more than 35

million private automobiles," H.H. Kelly, *United Nations Conference on Road and Motor Transport, A Report on the Preparation, Formulation, and Signature of a World Convention on Road Traffic*, US Department of State, Bulletin, Vol. XXI, No. 545 (December 12, 1949), 875a, which accounted for "more than 70 percent of all the motor vehicles in the world," *id.* "The largest volume of travel has been into Canada, Mexico, and Cuba, but ... about 3,000 United States cars [were] taken to Europe for touring purposes" in 1949 alone. *Id.*

[62] Specifically, the Sub-Committee on Road Transport of the Inland Transport Committee of the Economic Commission for Europe. Actually, both this draft and the 1943 Convention were designated as working papers for the conference, *see* United Nations Economic and Social Council, Report of the second session of the Transport and Communications Commission, Resolutions of 28 August 1948, E/1053 (28 August 1948), in Resolutions adopted by the Economic and Social Council during its seventh session from 19 July to 29 August 1948, E/1065/Corr.1 (11 March 1953), but the ECE document clearly served as the draft treaty.

[63] Economic Commission for Europe, Inland Transport Committee, Sub-Committee on Road Transport, *Draft Provisions for Insertion in a Convention on Road and Motor Transport, Explanatory Memorandum submitted by the Sub-Committee on Road Transport*, E/ECE/86 as corrected by E/ECE/86. Corr. 1 [hereinafter ECE Memo] at par. 3, contained in UK Ministry of Transport, *Draft Provisions for Insertion in a Convention on Road and Motor Transport and Explanatory Memorandum*, London (1949) [hereinafter UK Ministry of Transport].

[64] "Mr. PERLOWSKY (AIT/FIA) drew attention to the fact that the Draft Convention was based on the International Convention relative to Road Traffic and the International Convention relative to Motor Traffic, both signed in 1926, as well as on the Convention concerning the Unification of Road Signals, signed in 1931, the two latter of which contained provisions relating to national traffic." United Nations Economic and Social Council, United Nations Conference on Road and Motor Transport, Committee I on Legal and General Matters and Documents, *Summary Record of the First Meeting, Held at the Palais des Nations, Geneva, on Wednesday, 24 August 1949 at 3 p.m.*, E/CONF.8/C.1/SR.1 (24 August 1949) at 9 [Scan 18361].

[65] United Nations Economic and Social Council, United Nations Conference on Road and Motor Transport, Committee III on Road Traffic, *Summary Record of the Second Meeting, Held at the Palais des Nations, Geneva, on Thursday, 25 August 1949 at 10 a.m.*,

E/CONF.8/C.III/SR.2.Rev.1 (21 November 1949) at 4 [Scan 18527], 6 [Scan 18529]. At some point, the word "must" in clause one was changed to "shall" and the phrase "able and in a position to control" in clause five was changed to "able to control." How and when these changes occurred, however, is unclear.

[66] The French draft prepared for the 1926 Paris conference provided as follows (in a section entitled "Conduite des Véhicules, Bêtes de Charge ou de Trait et Animaux"):

> Art. 2. Tout véhicule doit avoir un conducteur; toutefois, un convoi de véhicules à traction animale peut ne comporter qu'un conducteur par trois véhicules à condition que les attelages du deuxième et du troisième soient attachés à l'arrière du véhicule qui les précède immédiatement.
>
> Les bêtes de trait ou de charge et les bestiaux en circulation sur la route doivent être accompagnés.
>
> Art. 3. Les conducteurs doivent être constamment en état et en position de diriger leur véhicule ou de guider leurs attelages, bêtes de trait, de charge ou bestiaux....

République Française, Ministère des Affaires Étrangères, Conférence Internationale relative à la Circulation Automobile et Routière, 1926 Paris, Imprimerie Nationale 1927, 197693.

[67] *See, e.g.*, 1926 Motor Traffic Convention, arts. 3 ("The controls and steering apparatus must be so placed that the driver can manage them with certainty and at the same time have a clear view of the road."), 6 ("The driver of a motor vehicle must possess qualifications which provide a reasonable guarantee of public safety....").

[68] Notably, cattle need only be "accompanied," and the division of convoys is not required "in regions where migration of nomads occurs." Geneva Convention, *supra* note 50, art. 8. As a representative from Iran explained, "it was customary for a very few men to drive hundreds or thousands of cattle...." E/CONF.8/C.III/SR.2.Rev.1, *supra* note 65, at 4 [Scan 18527].

[69] Normal Bel Geddes, Magic Motorways (1940) at 56. Later in the book, the author narrates how "the truckman *and his relief driver* climb aboard" their truck before undertaking a highly automated trip from Washington, D.C. to San Francisco that lasts merely 24 hours (and 15 pages). *Id.* at 152 (emphasis added).

[70] Kelly, *supra* note 61, at 879 ("[T]hese brief rules are only a selection of the basic requirements found in the elaborate traffic laws

and regulations of many countries, all of which have certain fundamentals in common."); United Nations Economic and Social Council, United Nations Conference on Road and Motor Transport, Committee I on Legal and General Matters and Documents, *Summary Record of the First Meeting, Held at the Palais des Nations, Geneva, on Wednesday, 24 August at 3 p.m.*, E/CONF.8/C.I/SR.1 (24 August 1949) at 10 [Scan 18362] ("Mr. RUMPLER (France) said that in drafting Chapter II the preparatory committees had consistently kept in mind the difficulties of federal states, and had consequently included therein only such rules as were uniformly and unanimously applied in the majority of countries."); UK Ministry of Transport, *supra* note 63, Introduction, par. 5 ("Most of the rules embodied in Chapter II conform with those in the Highway Code. There would be little change in the habits of British road users if this part of the Draft were accepted.").

[71] 1943 Convention, *supra* note 58, art. 2.

[72] *See* Uniform Veh. Code, Act V, Uniform Act Regulating Traffic on Highways (1939) § 10(c) ("Driver.—Every person who drives or is in actual physical control of a vehicle."); *see also* Uniform Veh. Code, Act II, Uniform Motor-Vehicle Operators' and Chauffeurs' License Act (1926) § 1(f) ("'Operator.' Every person, other than a chauffeur, who is in actual physical control of a motor vehicle upon a highway."); *infra* note 304.

[73] *ECE Memo*, *supra* note 63, *Draft Provisions to be Inserted in a Convention on Road and Motor Transport*, art. 4 par. 1.

[74] United Nations Economic and Social Council, United Nations Conference on Road and Motor Transport, Committee III on Road Traffic, *Summary Record of the Seventeenth Meeting, Held at the Palais des Nations, Geneva, on Tuesday, 6 September 1949 at 3 p.m.*, E/CONF.8/C.III/SR.17.Rev.1 (21 November 1949) at 2 [Scan 18536].

[75] *Id.*

[76] Geneva Convention, *supra* note 50, art. 4 (emphasis added).

[77] Geneva Convention, *supra* note 50, *Accessions and Ratifications*, treaties.un.org/pages/ViewDetailsV.aspx?&src=TREATY&mtdsg_no =XI~B~1&chapter=11&Temp=mtdsg5&lang=en.

[78] Albania, Austria, Belgium, Bulgaria, Central African Republic, Côte d'Ivoire (Ivory Coast), Cuba, Czech Republic, Democratic Republic of the Congo, Denmark, Finland, France, Georgia, Greece, Hungary, Israel, Italy, Kyrgyzstan, Luxembourg, Monaco, Montenegro, Morocco, Netherlands, Niger, Norway, Peru, Philippines, Poland,

Portugal, Romania, Russian Federation, San Marino, Senegal, Serbia, Slovakia, South Africa, Sweden, Tunisia, United Arab Emirates, and Zimbabwe. *Compare id. with* Convention on Road Traffic, Vienna, November 8, 1968, 1042 U.N.T.S. 17 (with subsequent amendments) [hereinafter Vienna Convention], *Accessions and Ratifications*, treaties.un.org/pages/ViewDetailsIII.aspx?&src=TREATY&mtdsg_no =XI~B~19&chapter=11&Temp=mtdsg3&lang=en.

[79] Also of note are, inter alia, (1) the European Agreement Supplementing the 1949 Convention on Road Traffic and the 1949 Protocol On Road Signs And Signals, signed at Geneva on 16 September 1950 and (2) the European Agreement Supplementing the Convention on Road Traffic opened for signature at Vienna on 8 November 1968. Article 8 of the Convention on International Civil Aviation addresses pilots instead of drivers: "No aircraft capable of being flown without a pilot shall be flown without a pilot over the territory of a contracting State without special authorization by that State and in accordance with the terms of such authorization. Each contracting State undertakes to insure that the flight of such aircraft without a pilot in regions open to civil aircraft shall be so controlled as to obviate danger to civil aircraft." Convention on International Civil Aviation, Chicago, December 1, 1944, art. 8.

[80] For background on the UNECE's work on road safety, see Kevin M. McDonald, *Shifting Out of Neutral: A New Approach to Global Road Safety*, 38 Vand. J. Transnat'l L. 743 2005. The Inland Transport Committee recently recognized a relationship between the two treaties in a different context. *See* Economic Commission for Europe, Inland Transport Committee, Working Party on Road Transport, *Annotated provisional agenda for the 106th session*, 25 July 2011, ECE/Trans/SC.1/395, www.unece.org/fileadmin/DAM/trans/doc/2011/sc1/ECE-TRANS-SC1-395e.pdf at I(4)(f).

[81] Vienna Convention, *supra* note 78, art. 8.

[82] *Id.*

[83] *Id.* art. 13. In contrast, the equivalent article in the Geneva Convention provides that "The driver of a vehicle shall at all times have its speed under control and shall drive in a reasonable and prudent manner. He shall slow down or stop whenever circumstances so require, and particularly when visibility is not good." Geneva Convention, *supra* note 50, art. 10.

[84] Vienna Convention, *supra* note 78, art. 1.

[85] *See supra* note 72.

[86] Vienna Convention, *supra* note 78, art. 1.

[87] *See* Clemens Arzt, Jana Eier, und Simone Ruth-Schumcher, Rechtliche Bewertung: Ordnungsrecht und Zulassungsrecht, in Gasser, *supra* note 34, at 54-55 (citing Economic Commission for Europe, TRANS/WP.1/2001/15, TRANSP/WP.1/2001/37, TRANSP/WP.1/2002/9).

[88] *Id.* at 54 ("[H]insichtlich des Systems [Intelligent Speed Adaption] wird aus deutscher Sicht eine Vereinbarkeit mit dem [Vienna Convention] nur für die Systemvarianten anerkannt, die jederzeit vom Fahrzeugführer übersteuert werden können.").

[89] *See* Gasser, *supra* note 34. The final report simply referenced the Vienna Convention in support of its broader conclusion that German law, in the abstract and in its application, requires a (human) driver to attentively monitor traffic and the roadway. *Id.* at 13.

[90] Arzt, *supra* note 87, at 54-55. There is some internal tension in the German position. On one hand, it holds that the Convention requires total human control; on the other hand, it assumes that a driver will abdicate that control when operating a vehicle that does not need her. *See* Gasser, *supra* note 34, at 14 (noting that any system can be configured in a way that technically enables a driver to perform her driving duties).

[91] The status of antitheft, alcolock, and other driving authorization systems is potentially disputed. *See* Torsten Janzyk, Verband der Automobilindustrie [German Association of the Automobile Industry], WP.1 Round Table meeting on March 19, 2012 at 7 (excluding these from the proposed definition of "driving assistance system").

[92] Whereas the Geneva Convention is authentic in English and French, *see* Geneva Convention, *supra* note 50, signature ("in the English and French languages, both texts authentic"), the Vienna Convention is authentic in Chinese, English, French, Russian, and Spanish, *see* Vienna Convention, *supra* note 78, art. 56. The Vienna Convention's Russian text, incidentally, requires every vehicle to have a driver who is always able to drive it. *Id.* art. 8.

[93] *See* Arzt, *supra* note 87, at 55. The German term "Kontrolle" would seem to capture these meanings. *Id.*

[94] *Id.* (citing Economic Commission for Europe, TRANS/WP.1/2001/37, TRANS/WP.1/2002/9). These positions predated paragraph 6 of article 8. *Id.* Sweden and the Netherlands are also parties to the Geneva Convention. *See supra* note 78.

[95] Economic Commission for Europe, Inland Transport Committee, Working Party on Road Safety, Sixty-first session, March 21-23, 2011, Geneva, *Informal Document 1*, www.unece.org/fileadmin/DAM/trans/doc/2011/wp1/Informal_docum ent_01e.pdf. Notably, Germany has taken the position that "driver" necessarily "means a natural person, not a system." *Note by the secretariat, Consistency between the Convention on Road Traffic, 1968, and the vehicle technical regulations*, ECE/Trans/WP.1/2009/2/Rev.1, www.unece.org/fileadmin/DAM/trans/doc/2010/wp1/ECE-TRANS-WP.1-2009-2-Rev.1.pdf (setting forth an earlier proposal as well as Germany's response).

[96] Economic Commission for Europe, Inland Transport Committee, Working Party on Road Traffic Safety, Sixty-third session, March 19-22, 2012, Geneva, *Informal document 7*, March 16, 2012, www.unece.org/fileadmin/DAM/trans/doc/2012/wp1/63-Informal-document-7e.pdf; Economic Commission for Europe, Inland Transport Committee, Working Party on Road Traffic Safety, Sixty-fourth session, September 24-27, 2012, Geneva, *Consistency between the Convention on Road Traffic (1968) and Vehicle Regulations*, www.unece.org/fileadmin/DAM/trans/doc/2012/wp1/ECE-TRANS-WP1-2012-8e.pdf; Working Party on Road Traffic Safety, Sixty-fourth session, September 24-27, 2012, Geneva, *Annotated provisional agenda for the sixty-fourth session*, www.unece.org/fileadmin/DAM/trans/doc/2012/wp1/ECE-TRANS-WP1-136e.pdf. Of some interest is Sweden's suggestion that "this wording is aimed at making the car manufacturers not liable if a [driver assistance system] does not work as intended and thinks that it's not appropriate to regulate this issue in the Convention." *Informal document 7, supra* note 96; *cf. also* Arzt, *supra* note 87, at 55 (noting that some states believed that Germany's concerns about the Vienna Convention go to liability rather than legality).

[97] *See infra* parts 6.2-6.3.

[98] *See supra* note 70.

[99] *See supra* note 72; *infra* note 304.

[100] Geneva Convention, *supra* note 50, art. 4.

[101] *Id.*

[102] *Cf. infra* part 6.1.4.

[103] *See, e.g.*, Marius Emberland, *The Human Rights of Companies, Exploring the Structure of ECHR Protection* (2006), fds.oup.com/www.oup.co.uk/pdf/0-19-928983-2.pdf.

[104] *See, e.g., id.* at 4 n.20; Convention for the Protection of Human Rights and Fundamental Freedoms at art. 1(1), art. 34; *cf.* Charter of Fundamental Rights of the European Union, art. 42. Germany's basic law also recognizes human and corporate persons. *See* Grundgesetz, art. 19 par. 3.

[105] *Cf. infra* part 6.1.2.

[106] Geneva Convention, *supra* note 50, art. 4.

[107] *See supra* note 95.

[108] Geneva Convention, *supra* note 50, *id.* arts. 11 par. 2, 12 par. 4.

[109] *Id.* art. 12 par. 4.

[110] Geneva Convention, *supra* note 50, art. 8 par. 5.

[111] *Id.* annex 6 part III(j)(2).

[112] *Id.* annex 6 part III(b); *see also infra* notes 417-418 (noting similar requirements under US state law).

[113] The treaty's first substantive rule of the road provides that "[e]very driver, pedestrian or other road user shall conduct himself in such a way as not to endanger or obstruct traffic; he shall avoid all behaviour that might cause damage to persons, or public or private property." Geneva Convention, *supra* note 50, art. 7.

[114] *See infra* part 4.4.1.

[115] *See infra* part 4.4.2.

[116] *See infra* part 4.4.3.

[117] *See infra* part 4.4.4.

[118] *See infra* parts 4.4.3-4.4.4.

[119] Vienna Convention on the Law of Treaties, *supra* note 21, art. 31.

[120] Geneva Convention, *supra* note 50, pmbl.

[121] Vienna Convention on the Law of Treaties, *supra* note 21, art. 31.

[122] Geneva Convention, *supra* note 50, art. 8.

[123] This suggests that "be[ing] able to control" is the same as "hav[ing] control."

[124] Geneva Convention, *supra* note 50, art. 8.

[125] Vienna Convention on the Law of Treaties, *supra* note 21, art. 32. One might reasonably respond that the Convention can simply be amended. *See infra* part 4.5.2.

[126] Geneva Convention, *supra* note 50, art. 8.

[127] *Control*, Oxford English Dictionary; cf. Controller, Oxford English Dictionary (discussing the fiscal, mechanical, and electronic meanings of this term). Contemporaneous definitions were similar. *See* Ohio v. Wilgus, 31 O.O. 443 (Ohio Ct. Com. Pl. 1945) (citing three dictionaries and fourteen judicial decisions).

[128] *Axcelis Technologies v. Applied Materials*, 66 U.S.P.Q.2d 1039, 2002 WL 31761283, No. CIV.A 01-10029DPW (Dist. Ct. D. Mass. Dec. 10, 2002) at 6.

[129] *See supra* part 4.1.

[130] *See* Geneva Convention, *supra* note 50, art. 9.

[131] *Id.* art. 10.

[132] In contrast, a vehicle must have a "strong steering apparatus" (or "appareil de direction robuste"). Geneva Convention, *supra* note 50, annex 6, part III(a).

[133] *Id.* art. 4.

[134] *Cf. infra* part 6.1.1.

[135] *Drive*, Oxford English Dictionary (providing as examples of the latter that "[t]he Queen drove yesterday afternoon" and "you had better take a cab and drive to London Bridge").

[136] *See* Arzt, *supra* note 87, at 55.

[137] International Law Commission, *Articles on State Responsibility*, art. 17, note 7.

[138] Geneva Convention, *supra* note 50, art. 4.

[139] "Four-wheel ABS senses if any of the four wheels is about to lock, and if so, it quickly releases the brakes on that wheel and lets it start rolling again. Cycles of releasing, holding and reapplying brakes are repeated many times per second. As long as the driver maintains firm pressure on the brake pedal, ABS will automatically modulate the pressure at the wheels at a level close to the optimum braking force short of lockup. ABS will enable the driver to steer while braking, prevent yawing due to rear-wheel lockup, and on many surfaces reduce stopping distances relative to a skidding vehicle." Charles J. Kahane and Jennifer N. Dang, *The Long-Term Effects of*

ABS in Passenger Cars and LTVs, August 2009, DOT HS 811 182, www-nrd.nhtsa.dot.gov/Pubs/811182.PDF, at 1.

[140] "ESC systems have sensors that monitor the speed of each wheel, the steering wheel angle, and the overall yaw rate and lateral acceleration of the vehicle. Data from the sensors are used to compare a driver's intended course with the vehicle's actual movement to detect when a driver is about to lose control of a vehicle and automatically intervene in split seconds by applying the brakes to individual wheels and possibly reducing engine torque to provide stability and help the driver stay on course." Jennifer N. Dang, *Evaluation Note, Preliminary Results Analyzing the Effectiveness of Electronic Stability Control (ESC) Systems*, September 2004, DOT HS 809 790, www.nhtsa.gov/cars/rules/regrev/evaluate/809790.html.

[141] 49 C.F.R. §§ 571.121, 571.126; Regulation (EC) No 661/2009 of the European Parliament and of the Council of 13 July 2009 concerning type-approval requirements for the general safety of motor vehicles, their trailers and systems, components and separate technical units intended therefor, art. 12; Australian Design Rule 31/02, Brake Systems for Passenger Cars.

[142] *See supra* notes 34-40.

[143] *See infra* parts 6.1.1, 6.2.2, 6.2.3 (discussing control).

[144] HR Rep No. 1383, 73d Cong, 2d Sess. 26 (1934), *quoted in* Edward Brodsky and M. Patricia Adamski, Law of Corporate Officers and Directors: Rights, Duties, and Liabilities, 16:3; *see also Laperriere v. Vesta Ins. Group, Inc.*, 526 F.3d 715, 722-23 (11th Cir. 2008) (*per curiam*) ("Congress recognized that it would be difficult, if not impossible, to enumerate or anticipate the many ways in which actual control may be exercised and expressly declined to define the term 'control,' leaving courts free to decide issues of control status on a case by case basis."), *quoted in* Brodsky and Adamski, *supra* note 144.

[145] SEC Rule 405, 17 C.F.R. § 230.405 and SEC Rule 12b-2(f), 17 C.F.R. § 240.12b-2(f), *quoted in* Brodsky and Adamski, *supra* note 144.

[146] Articles on State Responsibility, *supra* note 137, art.8 note (5) n.160; *see generally* art. 8 notes (3)-(5) and art. 17 notes (6)-(7); Antonio Cassese, *The Nicaragua and Tadić Tests Revisited in Light of the ICJ Judgment on Genocide in Bosnia*, 18 Eur. J. Int'l. L. 649 (2007), ejil.oxfordjournals.org/content/18/4/649.full.pdf+html.

[147] *Prosecutor v. Duško Tadič*, Appeals Chamber judgment, par. 132. This is similar to the ICJ's "effective control" test. *See* Cassese, *supra* note 146.

[148] In *Military and Paramilitary Activities in and against Nicaragua*, the ICJ had "distinguished between two classes of individuals not having the status of *de jure* organs of a state but nevertheless acting on behalf of that state: (1) those totally dependent on the foreign state – paid, equipped, generally supported by, and operating according to the 'planning and direction' of organs of that state ... [and] (2) persons who, although paid, financed and equipped by a foreign state, nonetheless retained a degree of independence of that state...." Cassese, *supra* note 146, at 652. It then used a test of "effective control" to conclude that alleged human rights violations were attributable to that foreign state (the United States) when committed by the first group but not when committed by the second group. *Id.*

The ICJ later rejected both the ITFY's critique and its "overall control test." *Case Concerning the Application of the Convention on the Prevention and Punishment of the Crime of Genocide (Bosnia and Herzegovina v. Serbia and Montenegro)*, February 26, 2007, par. 406.

[149] *Prosecutor v. Duško Tadič*, *supra* note 147, par. 117.

[150] *Id.* par. 131.

[151] *See infra* part 6.4.

[152] *Axcelis*, *supra* note 128, at 6.

[153] In this regard, see Geneva Convention, *supra* note 50, annex 6 part III(g) ("Every motor vehicle shall have an exhaust silencer in constant operation to prevent excessive or unusual noise, *the working of which cannot be interrupted by the driver while on the road.*") (emphasis added).

[154] *Id.* at pmbl.

[155] *See supra* part 4.4.1.

[156] *See supra* part 4.1.

[157] *See infra* part 4.5.1.

[158] *See infra* part 4.5.2.

[159] *See infra* part 4.5.3.

[160] *See infra* part 4.5.4.

[161] The summary record in its entirety is rather illuminating on this point.

[162] Geneva Convention, *supra* note 50, art. 1. The conference's legal committee formed a special working group to resolve interrelated disagreements about the content of article 1, the existence of article 6, and the title of the treaty. *See* United Nations Economic and Social Council, United Nations Conference on Road and Motor Transport, Committee I on Legal and General Matters and Documents, *Summary Record of the Second Meeting, Held at the Palais des Nations, Geneva, on Thursday, 25 August 1949, at 11 a.m.*, E/CONF.8/C.I/SR.2 (25 August 1949) at 3 [Scan 18371]. The group succeeded. *See* United Nations Economic and Social Council, United Nations Conference on Road and Motor Transport, Committee I on Legal and General Matters and Documents, *Summary Record of the Sixth Meeting, Held at the Palais des Nations, Geneva, on Monday, 29 August 1949, at 10 a.m.*, E/CONF.8/C.I/SR.6 (29 August 1949) at 2 [Scan 18374]; United Nations Economic and Social Council, United Nations Conference on Road and Motor Transport, Committee I on Legal and General Matters and Documents, *Summary Record of the Eighth Meeting, Held at the Palais des Nations, Geneva, on Wednesday, 31 August 1949, at 3 p.m.*, E/CONF.8/C.I/SR.8/Rev.1 (15 November 1949) at 2, 3, 5 [Scans 18380, 18382, 18383].

[163] United Nations Economic and Social Council, United Nations Conference on Road and Motor Transport, Committee I on Legal and General Matters and Documents, *Summary Record of the First Meeting, Held at the Palais des Nations, Geneva, on Wednesday, 24 August 1949, at 3 p.m.*, E/CONF.8/C.I/SR.1 (24 August 1949) at 8 [Scan 18360]. After the conference, the lead US negotiator wrote that "[s]ome of the delegations apparently desired to overlook the international character of the convention and to emphasize as its primary purpose the regulation of internal, domestic traffic." Kelly, *supra* note 61, at 877. This may explain, in part, the 1968 Vienna Convention. *See supra* part 4.2.

[164] E/CONF.8/C.I/SR.1, *supra* note 163, at 8-11 [Scans 18360, 18361, 18362, 18363]; *see also* E/CONF.8/C.II/SR.17/Rev.1, *supra* note 53, at 6-7 [Scans 18510, 18511] ("Mr. FAIRBANK (United States of America) stated that, though deferring to the United Kingdom representative's more detailed knowledge of the negotiations which had led up to the formulation of the Draft Convention, he doubted whether the intention had really been to draft rules of the road of strictly national application. The whole

purpose of the Convention was, after all, to establish regulations for international traffic....").

165 Kelly, *supra* note 61, at 878. Although Kelly implies that this was the consistent position of the United States, the records of the conference are at best ambivalent on this point.

166 E/CONF.8/C.III/SR.2.Rev.1, *supra* note 65, at 2-4 [Scans 18525, 18526, 18527].

167 *Id.*; *see also* United Nations Economic and Social Council, United Nations Conference on Road and Motor Transport, *Summary Record of the Second Meeting, held at the Palais des Nations, Geneva, on Thursday, 15 September [1949], at 3 p.m.*, E/CONF.8/SR.11 (15 September 1949) at 6 [Scan 18604] ("The PRESIDENT [of the conference] observed that, in his view, one of the objects of a Convention such as that which they hoped to sign was that certain changes in national laws should result from the adoption of the Convention's provisions."); Kelly, *supra* note 61, at 875a ("It is not anticipated that United States acceptance of the convention will require any changes in motor vehicle laws in this country, nor will it entail any additional expense to public authorities.").

168 United Nations Economic and Social Council, United Nations Conference on Road and Motor Transport, Committee I on Legal and General Matters and Documents, *Summary Record of the Second Meeting, Held at the Palais des Nations, Geneva, on Thursday, 25 August 1949, at 11 a.m.*, E/CONF.8/C.1/SR.2 (25 August 1949) at 4-6 [Scans 18366, 18367, 18369]; *see also* E/CONF.8/C.1/SR.1, *supra* note 64, at 11 [Scan 18363]; E/CONF.8/C.III/SR.2/Rev.1, *supra* note 65, at 2 [Scan 18519]. At least initially, this concern was not well understood by all the representatives. *See* E/CONF.8/C.1/SR.2, *supra* note 168, at 4-6 [Scans 18366, 18367, 18369] ("Mr. BEST (United Kingdom) thought that a misunderstanding had arisen as to the purport of the United Kingdom version. The difficulties of the United Kingdom delegation were connected with the form in which the rules of the road had been cast."). Even the UK delegation appears to have contributed to the confusion. *See* E/CONF.8/C.III/SR.2.Rev.1, *supra* note 65, at 2-4 [Scans 18525, 18526, 18527] ("Mr. GILLENDER (United Kingdom) said that he did not propose to submit amendments to each article. If Committee I decided, however, that the Convention, if adopted, required each country to enact the various articles as part of its domestic law, his delegation reserved its right to reconsider its position on the whole of Chapter II.").

[169] The text of this article is based on language in a UK proposal for article 1.

[170] *See* E/CONF.8/C.I/SR.2, *supra* note 166, at 6 [Scan 18369] ("Replying to the United Kingdom representative, the SECRETARY said that Chapter II contained provisions which should be made binding on road users. Any State which accepted Chapter II would be bound to take effective steps to ensure that traffic practice in their countries conformed to those provisions. There was, however, no implication that such rules should never be violated...."); Kelly, *supra* note 61, at 877-78 (describing the UK position and the US response).

[171] "There are almost as many ways of giving effect to international law as there are national legal systems." Eilen Denza, *The Relationship Between International and National Law*, International Law, 2nd ed., at 429.

[172] Vienna Convention on the Law of Treaties, *supra* note 21, art. 26 (*pacta sunt servanda*); *see Gabčíkovo-Nagymaros Project (Hungary/Slovakia), Judgment*, ICJ Reports 1997 at par. 114.

[173] Geneva Convention, *supra* note 50, art. 6.

[174] *Id.* art. 8.

[175] Articles on State Responsibility, *supra* note 137. The two potentially relevant circumstances are consent (in which the facially injured state agrees to the action) and necessity (in which the action "is the only means for the State to safeguard an essential interest against a grave and imminent peril"). *Id.*

[176] *Gabčíkovo-Nagymaros Project (Hungary/Slovakia), Judgment*, ICJ Reports 1997 at pars. 46-48; *Factory at Chorzów, Jurisdiction*, Judgment No. 8, 1927, PCIJ, Ser A, No. 9 at 21; *see generally* Articles on State Responsibility, *supra* note 137.

[177] *Factory, supra* note 176, at 21; *see* Articles on State Responsibility, *supra* note 137.

[178] The bills enacted in Nevada, Florida, and California do not reference the Geneva Convention. *See infra* part 6.4.

[179] Article 31's full procedure is more complex. A party may propose an amendment, and each party may vote on the amendment or request a conference. Ultimately, two-thirds of parties must vote to approve the amendment for it to become binding on all parties except those that have filed timely objections to it. This language appears to suggest that parties can thereby modify their obligations even to parties that object to the modification.

[180] Geneva Convention, *supra* note 50, art. 32.

[181] *See, e.g.*, ADAC, *Internationaler Führerschein – wann braucht man ihn*, www.adac.de/infotestrat/ratgeber-verkehr/fuehrerschein/internationaler-fuehrerschein/default.aspx?tabid=tab3 (not distinguishing between Geneva Convention parties and Vienna Convention parties). Germany was occupied at the time of the Geneva conference. Although it never ratified the Geneva Convention, it is a party to the Vienna Convention. In contrast, Japan—like the United States—is a party to the Geneva Convention but not to the Vienna Convention.

[182] UN Charter, art. 96 (advisory opinions), chap. X (ECOSOC), www.un.org/en/documents/charter/chapter14.shtml; ICJ Statute, art. 65; General Assembly Resolution 89(I), Authorization of the Economic and Social Council to request Advisory Opinions of the International Court of Justice, December 11, 1946, www.un.org/documents/ga/res/1/ares1.htm.

[183] *See* ECOSOC Res. 1989/75; ECOSOC Res. E/1998/L.49/Rev.1.

[184] They may also constitute a failure to act by the federal government, which can itself constitute state action.

[185] Whether natural or corporate. *See, e.g.*, *Barcelona Traction, Light and Power Company, Judgment*, ICJ Reports 1970 at 3, www.icj-cij.org/docket/files/50/5387.pdf.

[186] International Law Commission, Articles on Diplomatic Protection; *see also* E/CONF.8/C.I/SR.8/Rev.1, *supra* note 162, at 4 [Scan 18379] ("Mr. BEST (United Kingdom) said that ... [o]nly a Contracting State which considered that it suffered injury in the person of one of its citizens, could take proceedings against another Contracting State which had failed to apply the Convention....").

[187] Geneva Convention, *supra* note 50, art. 33.

[188] *See infra* part 4.5.3.1.

[189] *See infra* part 4.5.3.2.

[190] *See infra* part 4.5.3.3.

[191] *See infra* part 4.5.3.4.

[192] *See infra* part 4.5.3.2.

[193] In other words, that she must not act in a way that places the United States in violation of its treaty obligation.

[194] In other words, that she must not act in a way that places her state in violation of a treaty that is binding as federal law.

[195] As Justice Breyer recounts:

> In *Avena*, the ICJ expressed "great concern" that Oklahoma had set the date of execution for one of the Mexican nationals involved in the judgment, Osbaldo Torres, for May 18, 2004. Responding to *Avena*, the Oklahoma Court of Criminal Appeals stayed Torres' execution and ordered an evidentiary hearing on whether Torres had been prejudiced by the lack of consular notification. On the same day, the Governor of Oklahoma commuted Torres' death sentence to life without the possibility of parole, stressing that (1) the United States signed the Vienna Convention [on Consular Relations (1963)], (2) that treaty is "important in protecting the rights of American citizens abroad," (3) the ICJ ruled that Torres' rights had been violated, and (4) the US State Department urged his office to give careful consideration to the United States' treaty obligations.

Medellin v. Texas, 552 U.S. 491, 514, 128 S. Ct. 1346, 170 L. Ed. 2d 190 (2008) (Breyer, J., dissenting) (internal citations omitted); *cf. also Executive Order No. 13491, Ensuring Lawful Interrogations*, 74 Fed Reg. 4893 (January 22, 2009). Prudence may also reflect a more pragmatic desire to avoid protracted litigation.

[196] *Cf.* Gasser, *supra* note 34, at 13.

[197] *Murray v. The Charming Betsy*, 6 U.S. (2 Cranch) 64 (1804); *see generally* Curtis A. Bradley, *The Charming Betsy Canon and Separation of Powers: Rethinking the Interpretive Role of International Law*, 86 Georgetown L.J. 479 (1998).

[198] Although civil liability falls outside the scope of this article, these three cases are nonetheless illuminating. *Schofield v. Hertz Corporation* arose when Albertino Duriatti, in the course of a single day, arrived in the United States, presented an international driving permit to and rented a car from Hertz, and drove that car into William Schofield. *Schofield v. Hertz Corp.*, 201 Ga. App. 830, 830, 412 S.E.2d 853 (Ga. Ct. App. 1991). Schofield sued Hertz for negligent entrustment, arguing "that actual knowledge can be imputed to Hertz that Duriatti was incompetent to drive the vehicle he rented because ... the Hertz employee who assisted Duriatti violated Hertz's policy of obtaining a valid driver's license, in addition to an international driving permit, before renting to foreigners." *Id.* at 831. The appeals court held that this failure "cannot be the proximate cause of injury to Schofield," because "[r]egardless of what Duriatti presented to the Hertz employee before he rented an automobile, he had a valid license issued by Great Britain, which pursuant to the Convention on Road Traffic, allowed him to rent an automobile in this country and to

drive it without further examination." *Id.* at 831-32. (This premise is incorrect, or at least incomplete: Renting a vehicle is different than driving a vehicle, and the Geneva Convention does not by itself compel private companies to rent cars to foreigners.) Similarly (and under similar facts), the court in *Ortiz v. North Amherst Auto Rental, Inc.*, held that a rental company could reasonably use the international driving permit "as a representation of the fact that the driver has a driver's license." *Ortiz v. N. Amherst Auto Rental, Inc.*, 64 Mass. App. Ct. 499, 502, 834 N.E.2d 273 (Mass. App. Ct. 2005). The court explained that while the permit "itself does not confer driving privileges," it "may only be obtained if the holder already has a valid driver's license." *Id.* at 501. Finally, in *Eskew v. Young*, the court relied on *Schofield* to hold that a recreational vehicle rental company had no obligation to instruct its British customer on how to drive in the United States, because under the Geneva Convention that driver's "possession of a valid British driver's license enabled Cruise America to rent the RV to him without any further examination." *Eskew v. Young*, 992 F. Supp. 1049, 1052-53 (S.D. Ill. 1998). This case is particularly striking, because but for a possible difference in driving norms between the United States and the United Kingdom (where "it is customary for a driver to flash his headlights to signal that he is yielding the right-of-way"), the collision between the British driver and the plaintiff would not have occurred. *Id.* at 1050.

[199] *State v. Campos*, 899 N.E.2d 215, 216 (Ohio Hamilton Cty. Mun. Ct. 2005). The court ultimately concluded that Ohio law both (a) prohibited the defendant from driving without an Ohio license and (b) failed to specify any penalty for doing so. *Id.* at 216-17.

[200] *People v. Platts*, 274 Ill. App. 3d 753, 753, 655 N.E. 2d 300 (Ill. App. Ct. 1995). Notably, the defendant does not appear to have argued that the statute under which he was convicted unlawfully impaired his right to drive under the Convention. Instead, he unsuccessfully argued that "(1) Illinois failed to follow the notice provision of a treaty governing foreign drivers when [his] Illinois driver's license was revoked; (2) [his] Illinois revocation was terminated when he was issued a Canadian driver's license; and (3) [his] revocation ended when he returned to Canada." *Id.* at 754 (internal citations omitted), 755 (discussing Geneva Convention art. 24).

[201] As noted below, the US Congress can constitutionally enact a law that contravenes a treaty. *See infra* part 4.5.4.

[202] 5 U.S.C. § 706.

[203] *Rainbow Nav., Inc. v. Dep't of Navy*, 686 F. Supp. 354, 356 (D.D.C. 1988) (enjoining the Navy from undertaking certain procurement actions); *cf. also Comm. of U.S. Citizens Living in Nicaragua v. Reagan*, 859 F.2d 929, 942 (D.C. Cir. 1988) (recognizing the possibility of a treaty claim under the APA but rejecting it in this case because of a subsequent federal statute).

[204] Carlos Manuel Vázquez, *Laughing at Treaties*, 99 Colum. L. Rev. 2154, 2183 (1999); David Sloss, *The Domestication of International Human Rights: Non-Self-Executing Declarations and Human Rights Treaties*, 24 Yale J. Int'l L. 129, 216 (1999); Bryant Walker Smith, *International Obligations Enforceable as Agency Constraints* (on file with author).

[205] National Conference of Commissioners on Uniform State Laws, Revised Model State Administrative Procedure Act (2010) § 508(a)(3), www.japc.state.fl.us/publications/USAPA/MSAPA2010.pdf.

[206] Nev. Rev. Stat. § 233B.135(3).

[207] Cal. Gov. Code § 11342.1.

[208] Fla. Stat. § 120.56(1)(a).

[209] It is also at least somewhat distinct from standing, which is discussed below. *See infra* part 4.5.3.3.

[210] "A person suffering legal wrong because of agency action, or adversely affected or aggrieved by agency action within the meaning of a relevant statute, is entitled to judicial review thereof...." 5 U.S.C. § 702.

[211] *See supra* text accompanying note 202.

[212] "The district courts shall have original jurisdiction of all civil actions arising under the Constitution, laws, or treaties of the United States." 28 U.S.C. § 1331.

[213] The individual victim, however, might nonetheless be able to recover under the common law of tort or property.

[214] "Cause of action" is itself a confusing term often applied to describe both the authority and the legal theory. *See* David Sloss, *When Do Treaties Create Individually Enforceable Rights? The Supreme Court Ducks the Issue in Hamdan and Sanchez-Llamas*, 45 Columbia J. of Transnational L. 20, 30 (2006) ("In contemporary usage, lawyers and judges say that a statute, for example, creates a private right of action if it grants an individual plaintiff a right of access to court.").

[215] *Id.* at 71.

[216] In a footnote in *Medellin*, the Supreme Court remarked that "[e]ven when treaties are self-executing in the sense that they create federal law, the background presumption is that '[i]nternational agreements, even those directly benefiting private persons, generally do not create private rights or provide for a private cause of action in domestic courts.'" *Medellin, supra* note 195, at 506 n.3 (quoting 2 Restatement (Third) of Foreign Relations Law of the United States § 907, Comment a, p. 395 (1986)). One scholar convincingly discredits nearly every part of that footnote. *See* Carlos Manuel Vázquez, *Treaties as Law of the Land: The Supremacy Clause and the Judicial Enforcement of Treaties*, 122 Harv. L.R. 599, 626-27 n.131 (2008). For example, this "background presumption" is at most an empirical observation that most treaties of a certain type tend not to create such rights. *Id.* This is an important distinction: A high rate of criminal convictions, for example, does not imply a "background presumption" that criminal defendants are guilty.

[217] *See supra* note 198.

[218] *See infra* part 4.5.3.2.

[219] *See, e.g., Cort v. Ash*, 422 U.S. 66 (1975). Though not directly relevant, the opinion of the UK delegation to the Geneva Conference that the Convention "conferred no right on any individual to take proceedings against any State under the Convention" is notable:

> Mr. BEST (United Kingdom) said that the provision in paragraph (ii) of the text proposed by his delegation was incorporated in the text for Article 1 recommended by the Working Group, although perhaps, less explicitly. That text conferred no right on any individual to take proceedings against any State under the Convention. Only a Contracting State which considered that it suffered injury in the person of one of its citizens, could take proceedings against another Contracting State which had failed to apply the Convention; even had the provision in question not been included under international law any person finding himself in a country other than his own was obliged to comply with the laws of that State.

E/CONF.8/C.I/SR.8/Rev.1, *supra* note 162, at 4-5 [Scans 18379, 18380].

[220] *Indep. Living Ctr. of S. California, Inc. v. Maxwell-Jolly*, 572 F.3d 644 (9th Cir. 2009), *vacated and remanded sub nom. Douglas v. Indep. Living Ctr. of S. California, Inc.*, 132 S. Ct. 1204, 182 L. Ed. 2d 101 (2012).

[221] Justice Breyer, joined by Justices Kennedy, Ginsburg, Sotomayor, and Kagan.

[222] *Douglas, supra* note 220, at 1211.

[223] Chief Justice Roberts, joined by Justices Scalia, Thomas, and Alito.

[224] The dissenters also noted that deciding the broader question of "whether the Supremacy Clause can ever provide a private cause of action" is not necessary. *Douglas, supra* note 220, at 1212 (Roberts, C.J., dissenting).

[225] Provided that four other countries did as well. *See* Geneva Convention, *supra* note 50, art. 29.

[226] US constitution, art. II, § 2, cl. 2. President Harry S Truman submitted the treaty to the Senate, and the Senate gave its consent without any declaration that the treaty was non-self-executing. *See* Geneva Convention, 3 U.S.T. 3008, T.I.A.S. No. 2487.

[227] US constitution, art. VI cl. 2 (supremacy clause).

[228] *Medellin, supra* note 195, at 514 (*quoting Foster v. Neilson*, 27 U.S. 253, 314). International agreements are also divided into categories (treaties, congressional-executive agreements, agreements pursuant to treaties, and presidential agreements) that have distinct meanings within US law but not within international law. *See Treaties and Other International Agreements: The Role of the United States Senate* (2001), www.gpo.gov/fdsys/pkg/CPRT-106SPRT66922/pdf/CPRT-106SPRT66922.pdf .

[229] *Compare Medellin, supra* note 195, at 514-15 *with id.* at 508-09 (considering the nature of only art. 94 of the United Nations Charter rather than the entire Charter) ("We agree with this construction of Article 94. The Article is not a directive to domestic courts."); *see id.* at 538 (Breyer, J., dissenting); Jean d'Aspremont and Catherine Brölmann, *Challenging International Criminal Tribunals Before Domestic Courts*, in Challenging Acts of International Organizations Before National Courts, at 117 n.23 (discussing whether art. 94 is self-executing); Presumably, some provisions of a self-executing treaty are not directly enforceable (or enforced) for other reasons, such as justiciability or standing.

[230] *Medellin, supra* note 195, at 504. *But see* William J. Carter, Jr., *Treaties as Law and the Rule of Law: The Judicial Power to Compel Domestic Treaty Implementation*, 69 Maryland L.R. 344, 346 (2010), www.law.umaryland.edu/academics/journals/mdlr/print/articles/69_2-

344.pdf (arguing that non-self-executing treaties can obligate the United States domestically).

[231] Vázquez, *supra* note 216, at 645 (citing *United States v. Percheman*, 32 U.S. (7 Pet.) 51, 88-89 (1833)).

[232] *Medellin*, *supra* note 195, at 506-07 (internal quotations and citations omitted).

[233] James Crawford and Simon Olleson, *The nature and forms of international responsibility*, *in* Malcolm Evans, ed., International Law (2010).

[234] *See supra* part 4.1.

[235] Geneva Convention, *supra* note 50, art. 1.

[236] *Id.* art. 6.

[237] *See supra* part 4.5.1.

[238] *See* Kelly, *supra* note 61, at 875a.

[239] Article 8 contains eight of them. *See* Geneva Convention, *supra* note 50, art. 8.

[240] *See supra* note 54.

[241] *See* Kelly, *supra* note 61, at 879.

[242] *See infra* part 6.3.3.

[243] *Medellin*, 552 U.S. at 570 (Breyer, J., dissenting).

[244] *Schofield*, 201 Ga. App. at 832 (internal citations and quotations omitted). The third negligent entrustment case discussed above, *see supra* note 198, found "the *Schofield* opinion to be well reasoned and an accurate statement of the law." *Eskew*, 992 F. Supp. at 1053.

[245] *Campos*, 899 N.E.2d at 216. The relevant statute had an explicit exemption for nonresident drivers who possess a license from another US state but no explicit exemption for nonresident drivers who possess a license from a foreign country. *Id.*

[246] Letter from Catherine W. Brown, Assistant Legal Adviser for Consular Affairs, US Department of State, to Charles C. Olson, General Counsel, Prosecuting Attorney's Council of Georgia (Apr. 12, 2002), *quoted in* Sean D. Murphy, ed., *State Responsibility and Liability, Contemporary Practice of the United States Relating to International Law*, 96 Am. J. Intl. L. 706, 710.

[247] Geneva Convention, *supra* note 50, art. 6.

[248] *City of Santa Monica v. Stewart*, 24 Cal. Rptr. 3d 72, 84 (2005); *see also* Cal. Code Civ. Proc, § 367 ("Every action must be prosecuted in the name of the real party in interest."). Standing rules for the federal courts and each state's courts are not uniform.

[249] Geneva Convention, *supra* note 50, art. 1 par. 2.

[250] *See, e.g.*, Christopher O'Neill, *Legislating Under the Influence: Are Federal Highway Incentives Enough to Induce State Legislatures to Pass A 0.08 Blood Alcohol Concentration Standard?*, 28 Seton Hall Legis. J. 415 (2004); Robert E. King and Cass R. Sunstein, *Doing Without Speed Limits*, 79 B.U. L. Rev. 155, 158-59 (1999); *see also South Dakota v. Dole*, 483 U.S. 203, 207-08, 107 S. Ct. 2793, 97 L. Ed. 2d 171 (1987) (holding that Congress may constitutionally link some highway funding to a state's minimum drinking age).

[251] *See National Federation of Independent Business v. Sebelius*, 567 U.S. ___, 2012 WL 2427810 (2012).

[252] *Missouri v. Holland*, 252 U.S. 416 (1920).

[253] *Comm. of U.S. Citizens Living in Nicaragua v. Reagan*, 859 F.2d 929 (D.C. Cir. 1988).

[254] *See supra* part 4.5.2.

[255] *See* Emily K. Penney, *Is That Legal?: The United States' Unilateral Withdrawal from the Anti-Ballistic Missile Treaty*, 51 Cath. U. L. Rev. 1287 (2002).

[256] *See Medellin, supra* note 195; *cf. In the proceeding between The Loewen Group, Inc. and Raymond L. Loewen and United States of America, Case No. ARB(AF)/98/3, Award*, International Centre for Settlement of Investment Disputes, (June 26, 2003), www.state.gov/documents/organization/22094.pdf.

[257] *See infra* part 6.5.

[258] *See generally* 49 U.S.C. § 30101-30102, 30111; 49 C.F.R. §§ 501-599.

[259] 49 U.S.C. § 30102(a)(8) ("'[M]otor vehicle safety' means the performance of a motor vehicle or motor vehicle equipment in a way that protects the public against unreasonable risk of accidents occurring because of the design, construction, or performance of a motor vehicle, and against unreasonable risk of death or injury in an accident, and includes nonoperational safety of a motor vehicle."), (9) ("'[M]otor vehicle safety standard' means a minimum standard for motor vehicle or motor vehicle equipment performance.").

[260] *See* 49 U.S.C. §§ 30102 (definitions), 30112(a)(1) ("Except as [otherwise provided], a person may not manufacture for sale, sell, offer for sale, introduce or deliver for introduction in interstate commerce, or import into the United States, any motor vehicle or motor vehicle equipment manufactured on or after the date an applicable motor vehicle safety standard prescribed under this chapter takes effect unless the vehicle or equipment complies with the standard and is covered by a certification issued under section 30115 of this title."), (b) (excluding from this restriction "the sale, offer for sale, or introduction or delivery for introduction in interstate commerce of a motor vehicle or motor vehicle equipment after the first purchase of the vehicle or equipment in good faith other than for resale"), 30115 ("A manufacturer or distributor of a motor vehicle or motor vehicle equipment shall certify to the distributor or dealer at delivery that the vehicle or equipment complies with applicable motor vehicle safety standards prescribed under this chapter. A person may not issue the certificate if, in exercising reasonable care, the person has reason to know the certificate is false or misleading in a material respect. Certification of a vehicle must be shown by a label or tag permanently fixed to the vehicle. Certification of equipment may be shown by a label or tag on the equipment or on the outside of the container in which the equipment is delivered."); *see generally* 49 C.F.R. § 571; *see also* 49 U.S.C. § 30126 (requiring the promulgation of "uniform motor vehicle safety standards applicable to all used motor vehicles").

[261] A detailed analysis of NHTSA's statutory authority with respect to automated vehicles is likely forthcoming. *See* Steve Wood, *Federal Regulatory Issues Facing Autonomous Vehicles*, Santa Clara Law Review (2012). That authority may be broader in theory than in practice. *See* Jerry L. Mashaw and David L. Harfst, *Regulation and Legal Culture: The Case of Motor Vehicle Safety*, 4 Yale J. on Reg. 257 (Spring 1987) (arguing that the courts and Congress frustrated the agency's rulemaking and that NHTSA "legitimized its existence by abandoning its statutory mandate").

[262] *See, e.g.*, 49 C.F.R. § 571.101 ("Controls and displays") ("The purpose of this standard is to ensure the accessibility, visibility and recognition of motor vehicle controls, telltales and indicators, and to facilitate the proper selection of controls under daylight and nighttime conditions, in order to reduce the safety hazards caused by the diversion of the driver's attention from the driving task, and by mistakes in selecting controls."). In this way, the FMVSSs may compel the installation of unnecessary equipment on a fully automated vehicle.

[263] 49 C.F.R. § 571.3(b).

[264] *See generally* 49 C.F.R. § 571. Indeed, the safety standard for "[p]assenger car brake systems" references the electrical actuation of both service and parking brakes. 49 C.F.R. § 571.135 at S4 (defining "[e]lectrically-actuated service brakes" and "[s]plit service brake system"), S5.2 ("Each vehicle shall be equipped with a parking brake system of a friction type with solely mechanical means to retain engagement."), S5.5.1(e)-(f) (brake system warning indicator), S6.3.2 ("State of charge of batteries for electrically-actuated service brakes"), S7.10.3(f) (particular test procedure for hydraulic failure), S7.11.1 (particular test procedure for power failure), S7.12.2(i) (specific test procedure for parking brake).

[265] VINs must identify, inter alia, a vehicle's manufacturer as well as "[m]ake, line, series, body type, engine type, and all restraint devices and their location." 49 C.F.R. § 565. NHTSA may, at some point, expand the information communicated by the VIN, but it has yet to do so. *See* Vehicle Identification Number Requirements, Notice of Final Rulemaking, [Docket No. NHTSA 2008-0022], RIN 2127-AJ99 at 18 ("The agency is not adopting at this time amendments to address any of the recommendations for the VIN to include additional information elements, not because those recommendations lack merit, but instead because there is a pressing need for today's rule to be in place to assure the uninterrupted continuation of the VIN system.").

[266] NHTSA does not require the installation of EDRs but does regulate those that are installed. 49 C.F.R. § 563. Congress considered mandating EDRs in all new passenger vehicles as part of its reauthorization of highway funding, *see* SB 1813, § 31406, www.govtrack.us/congress/bills/112/s1813/text, but declined to do so in the final bill, *see* HR 4348 (MAP-21), www.gpo.gov/fdsys/pkg/BILLS-112hr4348enr/pdf/BILLS-112hr4348enr.pdf. The final bill does require "an examination of the need for safety standards with regard to electronic systems in passenger motor vehicles." *Id.* § 31402.

[267] Indeed, "event data do not include audio and video data." 49 C.F.R. § 563.

[268] 49 C.F.R. § 571.500.

[269] *See, e.g.,* Letter from John Womack, Acting Chief Counsel, NHTSA, to Richard King, Manager/Director, Wheel Lighting Devices, Ltd., July 5, 2001 ("Please note that the agency is growing increasingly conservative in its views about the permissibility under Federal law of novelty lighting items which have no discernable

safety benefit, given the possibility of these devices causing confusion to drivers and distracting them from the safety messages sent by required lighting equipment."); Letter from Stephen P. Wood, Acting Chief Counsel, NHTSA, to Herbert E. Stoel, April 8, 1990 ("We are learning that changes in lamp function, operation, and color should be approached in a conservative fashion, so as not to confuse the operators of other vehicles."); Letter from Frank Seales, Jr., Chief Counsel, NHTSA, to Richard S. Lugar, US Senate, May 9, 2000 ("Over the years we have come to believe that lamps must perform only their assigned function, and our interpretations of Standard No. 108 have become more conservative."); cf. also, e.g., NHTSA, NHTSA Illegal Lighting Crackdown Continues, Press Release, NHTSA 43-04, October 19, 2004, www.nhtsa.gov/nhtsa/announce/press/pressdisplay.cfm?year=2004& filename=pr43-04.html (describing a crackdown on illegal lighting rather than an illegal crackdown on lighting).

[270] 49 C.F.R. § 571.108 tbls. I, III.

[271] SAE Recommended Practice J910 (January 1966). Later versions of this document are not incorporated into a safety standard and are hence not legally binding.

indicate to the approaching driver the presence of a vehicular hazard.

[272] See Letter from John Womack, Acting Chief Counsel, NHTSA, to Paul Michelotti, PM Technology, February 15, 2001 ("We interpret 'driver controlled' as meaning that the hazard warning signal unit must be activated and deactivated by the driver and not by automatic means."); Letter from Frank Seales, Jr., Chief Counsel, NHTSA, to Eric Reed, February 29, 2000 ("An automatic activation of the hazard warning unit would not be 'driver controlled' and is therefore not permitted."); Letter from Jacqueline Glassman, Chief Counsel, NHTSA, to Ted Gaston, Director of Maintenance, Muncie Indiana Transit System, April 25, 2005 ("We have previously interpreted 'driver controlled' to mean that the hazard warning signal system must be activated and deactivated by the driver and not by automatic means...."); cf. also 49 C.F.R. § 571.108 S5.5.11(1) ("Any pair of lamps on the front of a passenger car, multipurpose passenger vehicle, truck, or bus, whether or not required by this standard, other than parking lamps or fog lamps, may be wired to be automatically activated, as determined by the manufacturer of the vehicle, in a steady burning state as daytime running lamps (DRLs) and to be automatically deactivated when the headlamp control is in any "on" position, and as otherwise determined by the manufacturer of the

vehicle, provided that each such lamp [meets certain requirements].").

[273] Letter from John Womack, *supra* note 272; *see, e.g.*, Letter from Frank Seales, Jr., Chief Counsel, NHTSA, to C. Thomas Terry, Director, Safety Affairs & Regulation, General Motors North America, May 26, 2000 (discussing the activation of service brakes by adaptive cruise control and electronic stability control systems).

[274] 49 C.F.R. § 571.108 tbls. I, III.

[275] SAE J945 (February 1966).

[276] SAE J1395 (April 1985).

[277] 49 C.F.R. § 571.108 S5.1.3.

[278] *Id.*

[279] *See* Letter from Samuel J. Dubbin, Chief Counsel, NHTSA, to Mark A. Evans, Photometric Engineer, Calcoast – ITL, April 12, 1996 (concluding that "no Federal motor vehicle safety standard ... applies" to "a rear fog anti-collision laser system" but noting that FMVSS 108 requires that the device not "impair the effectiveness of the [proximate] center lamp"); Letter from John Womack, Acting Chief Counsel, NHTSA, to Jacqueline Frohman, Chief Financial Officer, Astron Group, Inc., April 11, 2001 (stating that "[w]e have no requirements for fog lamps at this time," concluding that the laser-based rear fog lamp described would not impair required rear lighting equipment, and cautioning about the possibility of hazards to other drivers); Letter from Frank Seales, Jr., Chief Counsel, NHTSA, to [Redacted], June 19, 2000 (stating that a laser device that "would shine on the hood of a passing vehicle ... could create actual hazards"); *see also infra* notes 290, 497.

[280] 49 C.F.R. § 567.7.

[281] An "altered vehicle" is "a completed vehicle previously certified ... that has been altered other than by the addition, substitution, or removal of readily attachable components, such as mirrors or tire and rim assemblies, or by minor finishing operations such as painting, before the first purchase of the vehicle other than for resale, in such a manner as may affect the conformity of the vehicle with one or more Federal Motor Vehicle Safety Standard(s) or the validity of the vehicle's stated weight ratings or vehicle type classification." 49 C.F.R. § 567.3. An "alterer" is "a person who alters by addition, substitution, or removal of components (other than readily attachable components) a certified vehicle before the first purchase of the vehicle other than for resale." *Id.*

[282] 49 U.S.C § 30102(a)(8).

[283] *See generally* 49 U.S.C §§ 30101-30170.

[284] 49 U.S.C. §§ 30118-30120; *see also id.* § 30166(m)(3)(c) (possible defects).

[285] 49 U.S.C. § 30118(b).

[286] 49 U.S.C. § 30120(i).

[287] 49 U.S.C. § 30118(a).

[288] 49 U.S.C § 30102(a)(2).

[289] 49 U.S.C § 30102(a)(8).

[290] *See, e.g., Dedicated Short-Range Communications*, US Department of Transportation Research and Innovative Technology Administration   (RITA), www.its.dot.gov/factsheets/dsrc_factsheet.htm (DSRC); *supra* note 279 (LiDAR).

[291] *See* USDOT, *Federal Motor Carrier Safety Administration*, www.fmcsa.dot.gov/rules-regulations/rules-regulations.htm.

[292] *See* 49 C.F.R. §§ 11.101-102.

[293] *See generally* 49 C.F.R. § 11.

[294] This is why note 304, *infra*, takes up only six pages and not sixty.

[295] *See infra* part 6.1.

[296] *See infra* part 6.2.

[297] *See infra* part 6.3.

[298] *See infra* part 6.4.

[299] *See infra* part 6.5.

[300] *See infra* part 6.1.1.

[301] *See infra* part 6.1.2.

[302] *See infra* part 6.1.3.

[303] *See infra* part 6.1.4.

[304] *See, e.g.,* Uniform Veh. Code (2000) § 1-126 ("Driver – Every person who drives or is in actual physical control of a vehicle."); Uniform Veh. Code (1954) (consolidating previous acts) §§ 1-114 ("Driver.—Every person who drives or is in actual physical control of a vehicle."), 1-136 ("Operator.—Every person, other than a

chauffeur, who drives or is in actual physical control of a motor vehicle upon a highway or who is exercising control over or steering a vehicle being towed by a motor vehicle."); Uniform Veh. Code, Act V, Uniform Act Regulating Traffic on Highways (1952) § 10(c) ("Driver.—Every person who drives or is in actual physical control of a vehicle."), (1948) (same); (1944) § 10(c) (same), (1939) § 10(c) (same), (1926) (not defined); Uniform Veh. Code, Act II, Uniform Motor-Vehicle Operators' and Chauffeurs' License Act (1944) § 2(b) ("Operator.—Every person, other than a chauffeur, who drives or is in actual physical control of a motor vehicle upon a highway or who is exercising control over or steering a vehicle being towed by a motor vehicle."), (1926) § 1(f) ("'Operator.' Every person, other than a chauffeur, who is in actual physical control of a motor vehicle upon a highway."); Uniform Veh. Code, Uniform Act Regulating the Operation of Vehicles on Highways (1926) (not defined); Cal. Veh. Code § 305 ("A 'driver' is a person who drives or is in actual physical control of a vehicle. The term 'driver' does not include the tillerman or other person who, in an auxiliary capacity, assists the driver in the steering or operation of any articulated firefighting apparatus."); Tex. Transp. Code § 541.001(1) ("'Operator' means, as used in reference to a vehicle, a person who drives or has physical control of a vehicle."); N.Y. Veh. & Traf. Law § 113 ("Driver. Every person who operates or drives or is in actual physical control of a vehicle. Whenever the terms 'chauffeur' or 'operator' or 'chauffeur's license' or 'operator's license' are used in this chapter, such terms shall be deemed to mean driver and driver's license respectively."); Fla. Stat. § 316.003(10) ("DRIVER.—Any person who drives or is in actual physical control of a vehicle on a highway or who is exercising control of a vehicle or steering a vehicle being towed by a motor vehicle."); 625 Ill. Comp. Stat. 5/1-116 ("Driver. Every person who drives or is in actual physical control of a vehicle."), 1-154.2 ("Operator. Every person who operates or is in actual physical control of any device or vehicle whether motorized or propelled by human power."); 75 Pa. Cons. Stat. § 102 ("'Driver.' A person who drives or is in actual physical control of a vehicle."); Ohio Rev. Code § 4511.01(Y) ("'Driver or operator' means every person who drives or is in actual physical control of a vehicle, trackless trolley, or streetcar."), 4501.01(X) ("'Operator' includes any person who drives or operates a motor vehicle upon the public highways."); Mich. Comp. Laws § 257.13 ("'Driver' means every person who drives or is in actual physical control of a vehicle."); Ga. Code § 40-1-1(14) ("'Driver' means every person who drives or is in actual physical control of a vehicle."), 40-1-1(38) ("'Operator' means any person who drives or is in actual physical control of a motor vehicle."); N.C. Gen. Stat. § 20-4.01(7) ("Driver. – The operator of a vehicle, as defined in subdivision (25). The terms 'driver' and 'operator' and their cognates are synonymous."), 20-4.01(25) ("Operator. – A person in actual physical control of a vehicle which is in motion or which has the engine running. The terms 'operator' and 'driver' and their cognates are synonymous."); N.J. Stat. § 39:1-1 ("'Driver' means the rider or driver of a horse, bicycle or motorcycle or the driver or operator of a motor vehicle, unless otherwise specified."); Va. Code § 46.2-100 ("'Operator' or 'driver' means every person who either (i) drives or is in actual physical control of a motor vehicle on a highway or (ii) is exercising control over or steering a vehicle being towed by a motor vehicle."); Wash. Rev. Code § 46.04.370 ("'Operator or driver' means every person who drives or is in actual physical control of a vehicle."); Mass. Gen. Laws ch. 90, § 1 ("'Operator', any person who operates a motor vehicle or trackless trolley."); Ind. Code § 9-13-2-47 ("'Driver' means a person who drives or is in actual physical control of a vehicle."), 9-13-2-118(a) ("Except as provided in subsection (b), 'operator', when used in reference to a vehicle, means a person, other than a chauffeur or a public passenger chauffeur, who: (1) drives or is in actual physical control of a vehicle upon a highway; or (2) is exercising control over or steering a motor vehicle being towed by another vehicle. (b) 'Operator', for purposes of IC 9-25, means a person other than a chauffeur who is in actual physical control of a motor vehicle. As added by P.L.2-1991, SEC.1. Amended by P.L.125-2012, SEC.17."); Ariz. Rev. Stat. § 28-101.18 ("'Driver' means a person who drives or is in actual physical control of a vehicle."), 28-101 ("39. 'Operator' means a person who drives a motor vehicle on a highway, who is in actual physical control of a motor vehicle on a highway or who is exercising control over or steering a vehicle being towed by a motor vehicle."); Tenn. Code § 55-8-101(15) ("'Driver' means every person who drives or is in actual physical control of a vehicle;"), 55-8-101(39) ("'Operator' means every person, other than a chauffeur, who drives or is in actual physical control of a motor vehicle upon a highway or who is exercising control over or steering a vehicle being towed by a motor vehicle;"); Mo. Rev. Stat. § 300.010(10) ("'Driver', every person who drives or is in actual physical control of a vehicle;"); Md. Code Transp. § 11-115 ("'Driver' means any individual who drives a vehicle."), 11-142 ("'Operator', as used in reference to a vehicle, means driver, as defined in this subtitle."); Wis. Stat. § 340.01(41) ("'Operator' means a person who drives or is in actual physical control of a vehicle."); Minn. Stat. § 169.011 ("Subd. 24. Driver. 'Driver' means every person who drives or is in actual physical control of a vehicle."); Colo. Rev. Stat. § 42-1-102(27) ("'Driver' means every person, including a minor driver under the age of twenty-one years, who drives or is in actual physical control of a vehicle."); Ala. Code § 32-1-1.1(14) ("DRIVER. Every person who drives or is in actual physical control of a vehicle."); S.C. Code § 56-5-400 ("Every person who drives or is in actual physical control of a vehicle is a 'driver.'"); La. Rev. Stat. § 32:1(16) ("'Driver' means every person who drives or is in actual physical control of a vehicle."), 1(44) ("'Operator' means every person, other than a chauffeur, who drives or is in actual physical control of a motor vehicle upon a highway or who is exercising control over or steering a vehicle being towed by a motor vehicle."); Ky. Rev. Stat. § 189.010(7) ("'Operator' means the person in actual physical control of a vehicle."); Okla. Stat. tit. 47, § 1-114 ("Every person who drives or is in actual physical control of a vehicle."), 1-140 ("Every person, including a commercial operator or driver, as defined in Section 47-1-108 of this title, who operates, drives or is in actual physical control of a motor vehicle or who is exercising control over or steering a vehicle being towed by a motor vehicle."); P.R. Laws tit. 27, § 5001(31) ("Driver.-- Shall mean any person who drives or has physical control in the area of the steering wheel of a vehicle or motor vehicle. He/she shall be deemed to be an authorized driver when he/she has obtained a driving license, which is in effect."); Conn. Gen. Stat. § 14-1(25) ("'Driver' means any person who drives, operates or is in physical control of a commercial motor vehicle, or who is required to hold a commercial driver's license;"), 14-1(62) ("'Operator' means any person who operates a motor vehicle or who steers or directs the course of a motor vehicle being towed by another motor vehicle and includes a driver as defined in subdivision (25) of this section;"); Iowa Code § 321.1.48 ("'Operator' or 'driver' means every person who is in actual physical control of a motor vehicle upon a highway."); Miss. Code § 63-3-121(b) ("'Driver' means every person who drives or is in actual physical control of a vehicle."), 63-1-3(c) ("The term 'operator' means any person in actual physical control of a motor vehicle on the highway;"); Ark. Code § 27-16-204(a) ("'Driver' means every person who is in actual physical control of a motor vehicle upon a highway or who is exercising control over or steering a vehicle being towed by a motor vehicle. [registration]"), 27-49-208(c) ("'Driver' means every person who drives or is in actual physical control of a vehicle. [rules of road]"); Kan. Stat. § 8-1416 ("'Driver' means every person who drives or is in actual physical control of a vehicle."); Utah Code § 41-6a-102(39) ("'Operator' means a person who is in actual physical control of a vehicle."); Nev. Rev. Stat. § 484A.080 ("'Driver' means every person who drives or is in actual physical control of a vehicle."); N.M. Stat. § 66-1-4.4.K ("'driver' means every person who drives or is in actual physical control of a motor vehicle, including a motorcycle, upon a highway, who is exercising control over or steering a vehicle being towed by a motor vehicle or who operates or is in actual physical control of an off-highway motor vehicle;"), 66-1-4.13.E ("'operator' means driver, as defined in Section 66-1-4.4 NMSA 1978"); W. Va. Code § 17C-1-31 ("'Driver' means every person who drives or is in actual physical control of a vehicle."); Neb. Rev. Stat. § 60-642 ("Operator or driver shall mean any person who operates, drives, or is in actual physical control of a vehicle."); Idaho Code § 49-105(15) ("'Driver' means every person who drives or is in actual physical control of a vehicle."), 49-116(1) ("'Operator' means every person who is in actual physical control of a motor vehicle upon a highway or private property open to public use."); Haw. Rev. Stat. § 286-2 ("'Driver' means every person who drives, operates, or is in actual physical control of a motor vehicle in any place open to the general public for purposes of vehicular traffic or who is exercising control over or steering a vehicle being towed or pushed by a motor vehicle."); Me. Rev. Stat. tit. 29-a, § 101.22 ("'Driver' has the same meaning as 'operator' as defined in subsection 48."), 101.48 ("'Operator' means an individual who drives or is in control of a vehicle or who is exercising control over or steering a towed vehicle."); N.H. Rev. Stat. § 259:25 ("'Driver' shall mean a person who drives or is in actual physical control of a motor vehicle as defined in RSA 259:60 or an OHRV or snowmobile."); R.I. Gen. Laws § 31-1-17(c) ("'Driver' means any operator or chauffeur who drives or is in actual physical control of a vehicle."), (d) ("'Operator' means every person, other than a chauffeur, who drives or is in actual physical control of a motor vehicle upon a highway or who is exercising control over or steering a vehicle being towed by a motor vehicle."); Mont. Code § 61-1-101(20) ("'Driver' means a person who drives or is in actual physical control of a vehicle."), 61-1-101(51) ("'Operator' means a person who is in actual physical control of a motor vehicle."); Del. Code tit. 21, § 101(42) ("'Operator' includes every person who is in actual physical control of a motor vehicle upon a highway, except that for the purposes of Chapter 29 of this title the term 'operator' shall include a chauffeur."); S.D. Codified Laws tit. 32 (defining neither term); Alaska Admin. Code tit. 13 (defining neither term); N.D. Cent. Code § 39-01-01.16 ("'Driver' means every person who drives or is in actual physical control of a vehicle."), 39-01-01.49 ("'Operator' means every person who drives or is in actual physical control of a motor vehicle upon a highway or who is exercising control over or steering a vehicle being towed by a motor vehicle."); Vt. Stat. tit. 23, § 4(25) ("'Operator' shall include all persons 18 years of age or over, properly licensed to operate motor vehicles."); D.C. Code § 50-1501 (defining neither term); Wyo. Stat. § 31-5-102(x) ("'Driver' means every person who drives or is in actual physical control of a vehicle;"); Guam Code tit. 16, § 1102(f)

("A driver is a person who drives or is in actual physical control of a vehicle."), 1102(v) ("An operator is a person, other than a chauffeur, who drives or is in actual physical control of a motor vehicle upon a highway."); V.I. Code tit. 20, § 101 ("'operator' includes a chauffeur, driver, or any person operating a motor vehicle"); *see also* Model Traffic Ordinance for Municipalities (1962) § 1-11 ("Driver.—Every person who drives or is in actual physical control of a vehicle."), (1956) § 1-11 (same); Model Traffic Ordinance (1946) § 9(b) (same); Model Municipal Traffic Ordinance (1936) § 8(b) (same), (1930) § 1 ("Operator. Any person who is in actual physical control of a vehicle."); N.Y.C. Traffic Rules and Regulations, www.nyc.gov/html/dot/downloads/pdf/trafrule.pdf (not directly defining driver or operator); L.A. Mun. Code § 80.00(a) (incorporating definitions in the Cal. Veh. Code); Mun. Code of Chicago § 9-4-010 ("'Driver' means every person who operates or is in actual physical control of a vehicle.... 'Operator' means every person who operates or is in actual physical control of any device or vehicle whether motorized or propelled by human power."); Houston § 45-2 ("Driver means every person who drives or is in actual physical control of a vehicle."); Military Police, *Motor Vehicle Traffic Supervision*, Army Reg. 190-5,OPNAV 11200.5D, AFI 31-218(I), MCO 5110.1D, DLAR 5720.1 (May 22, 2006), www.apd.army.mil/pdffiles/r190_5.pdf at 36 ("Driver [means] [a]ny person who drives or is in physical control of a motor vehicle. A driver is in physical control when in position to control the motor vehicle, whether to regulate or restrain its operation or movement. For example, sitting in a parked car behind the steering wheel, keeping it in restraint or in a position to control its movement. The word 'driver' is interchangeable with the word 'operator.'"); 36 C.F.R. § 1.4 (National Park Service regulation) ("Operator means a person who operates, drives, controls, otherwise has charge of or is in actual physical control of a mechanical mode of transportation or any other mechanical equipment."); Stanford University Traffic and Parking Code (August 2011), transportation.stanford.edu/pdf/Stanford_University_Traffic_and_Par king_Code.pdf (not directly defining driver or operator); *cf. also* Navajo Nation Code tit. 14, § 105.K ("'Driver' means every person who drives or is in actual physical control of a motor vehicle, including a motor-driven cycle, upon a highway or any lands under the jurisdiction of the Navajo Nation or who is exercising control over or steering a vehicle being towed by a motor vehicle."), 105.AA ("'Operator' means a person other than a chauffeur, who drives or is in actual physical control over a motor vehicle upon a highway or who is exercising control over or steering a vehicle being towed by a motor vehicle or exercising control over a motor-driven cycle, all-terrain vehicle, moped, or recreational vehicle, upon a highway, roadway or any lands within the Navajo Nation."); *supra* part 4.3 (Geneva convention); *supra* note 263 (FMVSS).

[305] *Adler v. Dep't of Motor Vehicles*, 228 Cal. App. 3d 252, 258 (Cal. Ct. App. 1991).

[306] *Panopulos v. Maderis*, 47 Cal. 2d 337, 342 (Cal. 1956).

[307] *Fairman v. Mors*, 55 Cal. App. 2d 216, 219-20, 130 P.2d 448, 450-51 (Cal. Ct. App. 1942) (applying California guest statute) ("A driver is one who 'is in actual physical control of a vehicle.' An operator is one who directs or superintends it. [The plaintiff] neither actually controlled the movements of the roadster nor directed its course. One sitting behind a steering wheel of a towed car is utterly helpless so far as directing the course or conduct of such car. He is not the driver either in the statutory sense or in any sense. No amount of turning of the steering wheel by him will alter its course. The allegation that the roadster was towed warrants the inference that it had no power to propel itself. An automobile incapable of moving under its own power is not 'driven' by any of its occupants when being towed by another automobile.") (internal citations omitted).

[308] *Arellano v. Moreno*, 33 Cal. App. 3d 877, 882-83, 109 Cal. Rptr. 421, 425 (Ct. App. 1973). Presumably, the acquaintance who was steering the vehicle from the outside was also a driver. *See id.*

[309] *See id.*; *State Farm Mut. Auto. Ins. Co. v. Coughran*, 303 U.S. 485, 491 (1938) ("If, as found, the automobile was being jointly operated by the wife and the girl [then] the risk was not within the policy."); *People v. Yamat*, 475 Mich. 49, 51 (Mich. 2006) (applying the state's felonious driving statute to a passenger who grabbed the steering wheel). *But see State v. Myers*, 207 Iowa 555, 223 N.W. 166 (Iowa 1929) ("[O]nly one person can be engaged in the physical operation of a motor vehicle at one time....").

[310] *See generally* Joseph Bassano, et al., *Operate and drive; operation*, 60 C.J.S. Motor Vehicles § 11; Joseph Bassano, et al., *Operator and driver*, 60 C.J.S. Motor Vehicles § 12.

[311] *Atkinson v. State*, 331 Md. 199, 205 (Md. 1993).

[312] *Id.* at 205 n.4.

[313] *Id.* at 205 (quoting *Thomas v. State*, 277 Md. 314, 318, (Md. 1976) (quoting *McDuell v. State*, 231 A.2d 265, 267 (Del. 1967))). Maryland defined "drive" in 1977. *See* Md. Code Transp. § 11-114.

[314] *See Mercer v. Dep't of Motor Vehicles*, 53 Cal. 3d 753, 764 n.6, 765 n.8 (Cal. 1991) (noting this difference in interpreting the state's

drunk driving law). *But see People v. Nelson*, 200 Cal. App. 4th 1083 (Cal. Ct. App. 2011), review denied (Feb. 29, 2012) (holding that a driver whose vehicle is stopped at a red traffic signal is "driving" for the purpose of the state's cell phone law).

[315] *See* 625 Ill. Comp. 5/1-115.8 ("Drive. To drive, operate, or be in physical control of a motor vehicle."). Illinois courts did distinguish between "drive" and "physical control" prior to legislative enactment of this definition. *See, e.g., City of Naperville v. Watson*, 175 Ill. 2d 399, 402 (Ill. 1997).

[316] N.Y. Veh. & Traf. Law § 1229-c.3; *see also infra* note 339.

[317] Colo. Rev. Stat. § 42-4-237.

[318] *See supra* text accompanying nn. 17-20.

[319] *E.g., Atkinson*, 331 Md. at 209 ("[I]t is a generally accepted principle of statutory construction that a statute is to be read so that no word or phrase is 'rendered surplusage, superfluous, meaningless, or nugatory.'") (quoting *Management Personnel Servs. v. Sandefur*, 300 Md. 332, 341 (Md. 1984)). Presumably, no part of the phrase "surplusage, superfluous, meaningless, or nugatory" is "surplusage, superfluous, meaningless, or nugatory."

[320] *Adler*, 228 Cal. App. 3d at 258.

[321] *Panopulos*, 47 Cal. 2d at 342 ("It is significant that the statute defines driver to be one 'who drives' as distinguished from one 'who is driving.' One who is driving is, of course, also a driver and falls within the category of those who are 'in actual physical control of a vehicle.' Since the statute contemplates both as drivers it must be assumed that the Legislature intended that one not at a particular moment in actual control of a vehicle may also be deemed to be a driver.").

[322] *See generally* James O. Pearson, Jr., *What constitutes driving, operating, or being in control of motor vehicle for purposes of driving while intoxicated statute or ordinance*, 93 A.L.R.3d 7; Jonathan Layton, *Proof That Driver Was "Operating" Motor Vehicle While Intoxicated*, 61 Am. Jur. Proof of Facts 3d 115; *Mercer*, 53 Cal. 3d 753, 764-69 (describing judicial and legislative approaches and responses); Kimberley F. Scott, *"Driving" Under the Influence in California: Mercer v. Department of Motor Vehicles*, 28 Cal. W. L. Rev. 123, 128 (1992); David Salvin, *The "D" In DUI Stands for Driving, Doesn't It? (What Is "Driving" and Do You Know When You Are Doing It?)*, Orange County Law., January 2007, at 18; Robert F. Koets, William Lindsley, Sarah Newcomb, and Susan L. Thomas,

Meaning of "drive", 17 Cal. Jur. 3d Criminal Law: Crimes Against Admin. of Justice § 312.

[323] *Compare, e.g., Atkinson*, 331 Md. at 212 *with City of Naperville*, 175 Ill. 2d at 406.

[324] *See supra* note 322.

[325] Uniform Veh. Code (2000) §§ 1-123 ("Drive – to operate or be in physical control of a vehicle."), 1-125 ("Driven – to have operated or been in physical control of a vehicle."); 625 Ill. Comp. Stat. 5/1-115.8 ("Drive. To drive, operate, or be in physical control of a motor vehicle."); Ariz. Rev. Stat. § 28-101.17 ("'Drive' means to operate or be in actual physical control of a motor vehicle."); Mo. Rev. Stat. § 577.001.2 ("As used in this chapter, the term 'drive', 'driving', 'operates' or 'operating' means physically driving or operating a motor vehicle."); Md. Code Transp. § 11-114 ("'Drive' means to drive, operate, move, or be in actual physical control of a vehicle, including the exercise of control over or the steering of a vehicle being towed by a motor vehicle."); Wis. Stat. § 346.63(3) ("In this section [on drunk driving]: (a) 'Drive' means the exercise of physical control over the speed and direction of a motor vehicle while it is in motion."); Conn. Gen. Stat. § 14-1(24) ("'Drive' means to drive, operate or be in physical control of a motor vehicle, including a motor vehicle being towed by another;"); Neb. Rev. Stat. § 60-468 ("Drive shall mean to operate or be in the actual physical control of a motor vehicle."); Haw. Rev. Stat. § 286-2 ("'Drive' means to drive, operate, or be in physical control of a motor vehicle in any place open to the general public for purposes of vehicular traffic."); N.H. Rev. Stat. § 259:24 ("'Drive,' in all its moods and tenses, shall mean to operate or be in actual physical control of a motor vehicle, [off-highway recreational vehicle], or snowmobile.").

[326] *See Pearson, supra* note 322, § 2[a].

[327] *See supra* note 325.

[328] *Mercer*, 53 Cal. 3d at 765 n.9.

[329] Wis. Stat. § 346.63 (emphasis added).

[330] *Mercer*, 53 Cal. 3d 753 at 768.

[331] *Id.* at 763. *But see supra* note 314.

[332] 625 Ill. Comp. Stat. 5/1-154.1 ("Operate. To ride in or on, other than as a passenger, use or control in any manner the operation of any device or vehicle whether motorized or propelled by human power."); Ohio Rev. Code § 4511.01(HHH) ("'Operate' means to cause or have caused movement of a vehicle, streetcar, or trackless

trolley."); Mich. Comp. Laws § 257.35a ("'Operate' or 'operating' means being in actual physical control of a vehicle regardless of whether or not the person is licensed under this act as an operator or chauffeur."); Ind. Code § 9-13-2-117.5(a) ("'Operate', except as provided in subsection (b), means to navigate a vehicle. (b) 'Operate', for purposes of IC 9-31, means to navigate or otherwise use a motorboat. As added by P.L.71-1991, SEC.6. Amended by P.L.125-2012, SEC.16."); Mo. Rev. Stat. § 577.001.2 ("As used in this chapter, the term 'drive', 'driving', 'operates' or 'operating' means physically driving or operating a motor vehicle."); Md. Code Transp. § 11-141 ("'Operate', as used in reference to a vehicle, means to drive, as defined in this subtitle."); Wis. Stat. § 346.63(3) ("In this section [on drunk driving]: ... (b) 'Operate' means the physical manipulation or activation of any of the controls of a motor vehicle necessary to put it in motion."); Or. Rev. Stat. § 801.370 ("'Operation' means any operation, towing, pushing, movement or otherwise propelling."); Vt. Stat. tit. 23, § 4(24) ("'Operate,' 'operating' or 'operated' as applied to motor vehicles shall include 'drive,' 'driving' and 'driven' and shall also include an attempt to operate, and shall be construed to cover all matters and things connected with the presence and use of motor vehicles on the highway, whether they be in motion or at rest."); D.C. Code § 50-1501.01(10) ("The terms 'operate' and 'operated' shall include operating, moving, standing, or parking any motor vehicle or trailer on a public highway of the District of Columbia.").

[333] *See* Pearson, *supra* note 322, pt. B. The meaning of "operate" and its cognates has also been considered in other legal contexts, notably automobile liability policies and owner-liability statutes. *See generally* W. R. Habeeb, *Meaning of "operate" or "being operated" within clause of automobile liability policy limiting its coverage*, 51 A.L.R.2d 924; Marlene A. Attardo, *What Constitutes "Use" or "Operation" Within Statute Making Owner of Motor Vehicle Liable for Negligence in its Use or Operation*, 103 A.L.R.5th 339.

[334] Vt. Stat. tit. 23, § 4(24). This definition has a long history. *See State v. Lansing*, 184 A. 692, 694 (Vt. 1936).

[335] 625 Ill. Comp. Stat. 5/1-154.1.

[336] Ohio Rev. Code § 4511.01(HHH); *see also Columbus v. Freeman*, 181 Ohio App. 3d 320 (Ohio Ct. App. 2009) (discussing whether trial court improperly elaborated on this definition in instructions to jury).

[337] Ind. Code § 9-13-2-117.5(a).

[338] *See, e.g., State v. Ebert*, 871. A.2d 664, 669 (N.J. Sup. Ct. App. Div. 2005) ("The term 'operate' [in the drunk-driving statute] must be

given broad construction."); *State v. Mulcahy*, 107 N.J. 467, 478 n.4 (N.J. 1987) (describing "applications of [the] general rule that [may] strain its outer limits"). For relevant statutes, see *infra* parts 6.2-6.3. In Texas, for example, a person generally "may not operate a motor vehicle on a highway" without a valid driver's license. Tex. Transp. Code § 521.021. And in New Jersey, "it shall be unlawful for any person to drive or operate a motor vehicle in an unsafe manner likely to endanger a person or property." N.J. Stat. § 39:4-97.2.

[339] *See* Pearson, *supra* note 322, pt. B; *People v. Hakimi-Fard*, 137 Misc. 2d 116, 117, (N.Y. City Ct. 1987) ("A person 'operates' a motor vehicle when he begins to use the mechanisms of the automobile for the purpose of putting the automobile in motion."); *accord* Wis. Stat. § 346.63(3)(b) (defining "[o]perate" for the purpose of the state's drunk driving statute as "the physical manipulation or activation of any of the controls of a motor vehicle necessary to put it in motion"). The phrase "inchoate driving" assumes a narrow definition of driving. *See supra* part 3.

[340] Pearson, *supra* note 322, § 3[b].

[341] *Commonwealth v. Uski*, 263 Mass. 22, 24 (Mass. 1928); *accord, e.g.*, *People v. Prescott*, 95 N.Y.2d 655, 662 (N.Y. 2001); *State v. Donaldson*, 663 N.W.2d 882, 887 (Iowa 2003) (theft of van); *State v. Morris*, 666 A.2d 419, 419 (R.I. 1995) (driving on suspended license).

[342] *People v. Wood*, 450 Mich. 399, 404-05 (1995).

[343] *But cf. Anderson v. Mehaidli*, 83 F.3d 422 (unpublished decision) (applying Michigan law) (declining to find operation in part because the individual was not "in or near the vehicle while the engine was running at the time of the accident").

[344] *See supra* note 341.

[345] *See Witherstine v. Employers' Liab. Assur. Corp., Ltd., of London, Eng.*, 235 N.Y. 168 (N.Y. 1923) (interpreting the phrase "operated by" in an automobile insurance policy); *Brown v. Ohio Cas. Ins. Co.*, 409 N.E.2d 253, 257 (Ohio Ct. App. 1978); *Le v. Vaknin*, 722 N.W.2d 412, 415 (Iowa 2006); *Twogood v. American Farmers Mutual Automobile Insurance Ass'n*, 296 N.W. 239, 242 (Iowa 1941) ("This does not mean that one who has general authority over a driver with respect to the destination, route, or rate of speed of the vehicle, is operating the vehicle."); *Elgar v. National Continental/Progressive Insurance Co.*, 849 A.2d 324, 327-28 (R.I. 2004).

[346] *Witherstine*, 235 N.Y. at 171-72 ("A surgeon operates when he amputates a patient's leg; a railroad company operates its railroad. The Workmen's Compensation Law provides compensation for injuries sustained by employees of those who are engaged in the business of operating vehicles on the street. Under the Labor Law the words 'to operate a machine' mean 'to regulate and control its management or operation.'") (internal citations omitted); *see also* Tex. Transp. Code § 542.002 ("A provision of this subtitle applicable to an operator of a vehicle applies to the operator of a *vehicle owned or operated by the United States*, this state, or a political subdivision of this state, except as specifically provided otherwise by this subtitle for an authorized emergency vehicle.") (emphasis added).

[347] *Id.* at 172 (internal citations omitted). Nine years later, however, the court did extend the meaning of "operation" in the state's owner-liability statute. *See Arcara v. Moresse*, 258 N.Y. 211 (N.Y. 1932); *see also N. v. Kolomyjec*, 199 Mich. App. 724, 726 (Mich. Ct. App. 1993) ("The purpose of [such a] statute is to place the risk of damage or injury on the person who has the ultimate control of the motor vehicle, as well as on the person who is in immediate control."). In *Arcara*, the vehicle's owner loaned his car to his nephew, who in violation of his uncle's express instructions permitted his friend to drive while he rode as passenger. *Arcara*, 258 N.Y. at 213. Perhaps unsurprisingly, that friend then crashed the car, and his victims sought compensation from the uncle under the common statutory provision that a motor vehicle's owner is liable for injuries "'resulting from negligence in the operation of such motor vehicle ... by any person legally using or operating the same with the permission, express or implied, of such owner.'" *Id.* at 213 (quoting the state's owner-liability statute). After determining that the uncle's proscription "related to the operation of the car, not to the use which might be made of it," *id.* at 214, the court held that "the legal user [i.e., the owner's nephew] may be guilty of negligence in 'operation,' though not 'operating' the car, in the sense that he is driving with his own hands. The clear implication is that, if the legal user at the time be present in the car, still 'the director of the enterprise,' still 'the master of the ship,' the operation of the car is his operation, though the hands at the wheel are those of a substitute, and the negligent driving will bind the owner, with whose permission the car is used." *Id.* (quoting *Grant v. Knepper*, 245 N. Y. 158, 165 (N.Y. 1927) (Cardozo, J.)). Similar cases have found permissive "use" by a person not even present in the vehicle. *See* Attardo, *supra* note 333, § 3 (discussing additional owner-liability cases); *Neel v. Indemnity Ins. Co. of North America*, 122 N.J.L. 560, 562 (N.J. 1939) (interpreting the phrase "while riding in or operating" an automobile in

an automobile liability policy to mean that "a person who is 'operating' a car is not necessarily the one who is 'riding in' it"). *But see* Habeeb, *supra* note 333, § 3 (discussing contrary insurance decisions).

[348] *State v. Ruona*, 133 Mont. 243, 248 (Mont. 1958) (combining definitions from Webster's New International Dictionary (2d ed.)). A more precise version would refer to "existing bodily restraint or existing bodily directing influence or existing bodily domination or existing bodily regulation or present bodily restraint or present bodily directing influence or present bodily domination or present bodily regulation."

[349] *In re Standard Jury Instructions in Criminal Cases*, 958 So. 2d 361, 362-63 (Fla. 2007); *see also Jackson v. Moore*, 883 P.2d 622, 626 (Colo. Ct. App. 1994) (holding that operation requires more than just actual physical control); *State v. Osgood*, 135 N.H. 436, 437, 605 A.2d 1071, 1072 (N.H. 1992) ("Nothing in the statute requires that a motor vehicle actually be operable in order for an individual to 'drive' it."); *Bearden v. State*, 430 P.2d 844, 845 (Okla. Ct. Crim. App. 1967) ("Defendant, who was lying unconscious at the side of the road, outside his vehicle; cannot be said to have existing or present bodily restraint, directing influence, domination or regulation of an automobile, while under the influence of intoxicating liquor; and cannot be said to be in 'actual physical control'; and, therefore, could not commit an offense within the provisions of the statute.") (from court syllabus).

[350] Ohio Rev. Code § 4511.194 ("'Physical control' means being in the driver's position of the front seat of a vehicle or in the driver's position of a streetcar or trackless trolley and having possession of the vehicle's, streetcar's, or trackless trolley's ignition key or other ignition device.") (codifying *City of Cincinnati v. Kelley*, 351 N.E.2d 85, 87 (Ohio 1976)); Idaho Code § 18-8002(7) ("'Actual physical control' as used in this section and section 18-8002A, Idaho Code, shall be defined as being in the driver's position of the motor vehicle with the motor running or with the motor vehicle moving."). *But see Cagle v. City of Gadsden*, 495 So. 2d 1144, 1145-46 (Ala. 1986) (criticizing these criteria as easily avoidable).

[351] *Cagle*, 495 So. 2d at 1145; *Atkinson*, 331 Md. at 210; *State v. Prawitt*, 262 P.3d 1203, 1208 (Utah Ct. App. 2011).

[352] N.M. Uniform Jury Instructions § 14-4512.

[353] *See* Uniform Veh. Code § 1-169; Cal. Veh. Code § 470; Tex. Transp. Code § 541.001(4); Fla. Stat. § 316.003(29); 625 Ill. Comp. 5/1-159; 75 Pa. Cons. Stat. § 102; Ohio Rev. Code § 4511.01(W);

Mich. Comp. Laws § 257.40; Ga. Code § 40-1-1(43); N.C. Gen. Stat. § 20-4.01(28); N.J. Stat. § 39:1-1; Wash. Rev. Code § 46.04.405; Mass. Gen. Laws ch. 90, § 1; Ind. Code § 9-13-2-124(a); Tenn. Code § 55-8-101(43); Mo. Rev. Stat. § 300.010(23); Minn. Stat. § 169.011.54; Colo. Rev. Stat. § 42-1-102(69); Ala. Code § 32-1-1.1(42); Okla. Stat. tit. 47, § 1-144; P.R. Laws tit. 27, § 5001(74); Conn. Gen. Stat. § 14-1(69); Miss. Code § 63-3-121(a); Ark. Code § 27-16-204, 27-49-208(c); Kan. Stat. § 8-1447; Utah Code § 41-6a-102(44); N.M. Stat. § 66-1-4.14.E; W. Va. Code § 17C-1-29; Idaho Code § 49-117(7)(a); Me. Rev. Stat. tit. 29-a, § 101.54; N.H. Rev. Stat. § 259:74, 21:9; Mont. Code § 61-1-101(53); Del. Code tit. 21, § 101(47); N.D. Cent. Code § 39-01-01.55; Vt. Stat. tit. 23, § 4(27); Guam Code tit. 16, § 1102(x); *see also* Navajo Nation Code tit. 14, § 105.FF; *see generally* Joseph Bassano, et al., *Operator and driver*, 60 C.J.S. Motor Vehicles § 12. *But see* Md. Code Transp. § 11-115 ("'Driver' means any *individual* who drives a vehicle.") (emphasis added).

[354] *See* Uniform Veh. Code, Uniform Motor Vehicle Registration Act (1926) § 1(p), Uniform Motor Vehicle Anti-Theft Act (1926) § 1(d), Uniform Motor-Vehicle Operators' and Chauffeurs' License Act (1926) § 1(d), Uniform Act Regulating the Operation of Vehicles on Highways (1926) § 1(l). The definition makes sense for some but not all of these constituent acts.

[355] *See, e.g.*, Tex. Transp. Code § 542.002 ("A provision of this subtitle applicable to an operator of a vehicle applies to the operator of a vehicle owned or operated by the United States, this state, or a political subdivision of this state, except as specifically provided otherwise by this subtitle for an authorized emergency vehicle."); Md. Code Transp. § 21-1107(c)(3) (excluding from a prohibition on riding in a vehicle's cargo area persons in "[a] vehicle owned or operated by the U.S. Department of Defense if the vehicle is controlled or operated by: (i) Active duty military personnel...").

[356] *See infra* part 6.4.

[357] Paul J. Becker, Arthur J. Jipson, and Alan S. Bruce, *State of Indiana v. Ford Motor Company Revisited*, 26 Am. J. Crim. Just. 181 (2002); James W. Harlow, *Corporate Criminal Liability for Homicide: A Statutory Framework, Note*, 61 Duke L.J. 123 (2011); Michael Willats, *Death by Reckless Design: The Need for Stricter Criminal Statutes for Engineering-Related Homicides*, 58 Cath. U. L.R. 567 (2009). Literature in this area sometimes conflates the prosecution of companies with the prosecution of individuals within those companies.

[358] *See supra* note 347.

[359] This is in addition to civil liability. *See, e.g.*, Sarah E. Williams, *Florida's Dangerous Instrumentality Doctrine*, 25 Stetson L. Rev. 177 (1995) (discussing the unusually broad civil liability of vehicle owners in Florida); Cal. Veh. Code § 17150 ("Every owner of a motor vehicle is liable and responsible for death or injury to person or property resulting from a negligent or wrongful act or omission in the operation of the motor vehicle, in the business of the owner or otherwise, by any person using or operating the same with the permission, express or implied, of the owner."); N.Y. Veh. & Traf. Law § 388 (same); Mich. Comp. Laws § 257.401(1) ("The owner of a motor vehicle is liable for an injury caused by the negligent operation of the motor vehicle whether the negligence consists of a violation of a statute of this state or the ordinary care standard required by common law.").

[360] Wash. Rev. Code § 46.16A.500.

[361] *See, e.g.*, Ga. Code § 40-6-20 (red light cameras); N.J. Stat. § 39:4-129(e) (injury crashes).

[362] *See* Wis. Stat. §§ 346.175 (fleeing traffic officer), 346.195 (failing to yield to authorized emergency vehicle), 346.205 (failing to yield to funeral procession), 346.452 (crossing railroad tracks), 346.457 (passing fire truck), 346.465 (crossing school crossing), 346.485 (passing school bus), 346.945 (radios).

[363] *See, e.g.*, Tex. Transp. Code § 542.302; Ohio Rev. Code § 4511.203; Mass. Gen. Laws ch. 90, § 12.

[364] *See infra* part 6.2.3.

[365] This is why the "driver" of a chauffeured vehicle is the chauffeur rather than the owner who rides in it. *See supra* note 345.

[366] *See, e.g.*, Pearson, *supra* note 322, § 8 (discussing persons sitting in stationary cars); *see also infra* part 6.4.3 (discussing California's autonomous driving statute).

[367] *See supra* part 3.

[368] *See supra* note 42.

[369] *See, e.g.*, *Escola v. Coca-Cola Bottling Co.*, 24 Cal.2d 453 (1944); *Greenman v. Yuba Power Products*, 59 Cal. 2d 57 (1963).

[370] *See* Alan C. Michaels, *Constitutional Innocence*, 112 Harvard Law Review 828 (1999); *Reference re Section 94(2) of the Motor Vehicle Act*, 2 S.C.R. 486 (Canada 1985).

[371] *See supra* part 6.1.3; Cal. Veh. Code § 17150 ("Every owner of a motor vehicle is liable and responsible for death or injury to person or property resulting from a negligent or wrongful act or omission in the operation of the motor vehicle, in the business of the owner or otherwise, by any person using or operating the same with the permission, express or implied, of the owner.").

[372] Ramona C. Rains, *Clemmons v. Fidler: Is Man's Best Friend A Landlord's Worst Enemy?*, 19 Am. J. Trial Advoc. 197 (1995); *cf. also* Geneva Convention, *supra* note 50, art. 8.

[373] *See, e.g.*, Mark E. Roszkowski, Christie L. Roszkowski, *Making Sense of Respondeat Superior: An Integrated Approach for Both Negligent and Intentional Conduct*, 14 S. Cal. Rev. L. & Women's Stud. 235 (2005).

[374] These are so-called public welfare crimes often related to financial disclosure, environmental protection, and consumer safety. Aaron F. Kass, *Mindless Guilt: Negative Aspects of State Environmental Prosecutions Using the Public Welfare Exception*, 29 Wm. & Mary Envtl. L. & Pol'y Rev. 517 (2005).

[375] *See, e.g.*, Cal. Veh. Code § 40000.1 ("Except as otherwise provided in this article, it is unlawful and constitutes an infraction for any person to violate, or fail to comply with any provision of this code, or any local ordinance adopted pursuant to this code."); Oreg. Rev. Stat. §§ 161.095 (establishing a minimum level of culpability for criminal liability), 161.105 (excluding violations from this requirement).

[376] *Panopulos*, 47 Cal. 2d at 342. *But see* Cal. Veh. Code § 21701 ("No person shall wilfully interfere with the driver of a vehicle or with the mechanism thereof in such manner as to affect the driver's control of the vehicle."). The distinction between status and conduct arises elsewhere in the law. *See, e.g.*, *Nielsen v. Moroni Feed Co.*, 162 F.3d 604, 608-09 (10th Cir. 1998) (recognizing a statutory "dichotomy between a disability and disability-caused misconduct ... where the disability is related to alcoholism or illegal drug use"); European Court of Human Rights App no 26629/95, Judgment of 4 April 2000, *supra* note 25 (interpreting the term "alcoholics").

[377] *See supra* part 6.1.2.

[378] *See infra* part 6.4.

[379] In the securities fraud context, there are three "competing theories" to determining whether a defendant controlled those who committed the primary fraud. *See* Laura Greco, Note, *The Buck Stops Where?: Defining Controlling Person Liability*, 73 S. Cal. L.

Rev. 169, 173-185 (1999). The first "determines who controls by looking at the individual's position in the company and ... relationship with the person or entity liable for the primary violation." *Id.* at 173. The second requires an additional finding that the individual was "'in some meaningful sense [a] culpable participant[] in the fraud perpetrated by controlled persons.'" *Id.* at 176 (quoting and modifying *Lanza v. Drexel*, 479 F.2d 1277, 1299 (2d Cir. 1973)). The third "consider[s] the power or potential power of an individual to control another person's activities, even if that power was not actually exercised." *Id.* at 180.

[380] Cal. Veh. Code § 21702.

[381] Elevator regulations offer an interesting analogy. *See, e.g.*, Massachusetts General Laws ch. 143 § 71G ("No person shall work as an elevator operator unless he has received a license therefor from the commissioner of public safety."); Ohio Rev. Code § 4105.14 ("Any person, firm, or corporation operating a passenger elevator shall provide a seat for the use of the operator of such elevator."); Minn. Stat. §§ 326B.169 (requiring designation of a "competent person or competent persons regularly to operate" "a passenger or freight elevator"), 326B.163 (excluding from the definition of "[p]assenger or freight elevator" any elevator that complies with safety rules and has "automatic operation or continuous pressure operation"); N.Y. Lab. Law § 203-a ("Every passenger elevator operated and maintained for use by the public shall be equipped or furnished with a seat, collapsible or otherwise, for the use of the operator when the elevator is not being operated [unless certain conditions apply].").

[382] *E.g.*, Cal. Veh. Code § 22350; *see infra* notes 435, 503.

[383] Nevada DMV, *Pre-Draft* (September 15, 2011) at 6 (on file with author).

[384] *See supra* part 6.1.3.

[385] *See supra* part 2.

[386] *See, e.g.*, *Truchan v. Nissan Motor Corp. in U.S.A.*, 316 N.J. Super. 554, 720 A.2d 981 (N.J. App. 1998).

[387] *See, e.g.*, *Wilding v. Norton* 156 Cal.App.2d 374, 379, 319 P.2d 440 (Cal. App. 1957)

[388] *See infra* part 6.2.1.

[389] *See infra* part 6.2.2.

[390] *See infra* part 6.2.3. Similarly, NHTSA does not require event data recorders (EDRs), but it does impose requirements on those EDRs that are installed. *See supra* note 266; *see also infra* note 381 (discussing elevators).

[391] Cal. Veh. Code § 12500 (specifying certain exceptions); *see also* Uniform Veh. Code § 6-101 ("Drivers must be licensed."). Notably, California's requirement also applies to "offstreet parking facilit[ies]." However, "[a] peace officer shall not stop a vehicle for the sole reason of determining whether the driver is properly licensed." Cal. Veh. Code § 14607.6.

[392] Cal. Veh. Code § 14604; *see* Uniform Veh. Code § 11-1603; *see also id.* § 6-305 (extending this prohibition to authorizing a vehicle to be driven "in violation of any of the provisions of this chapter").

[393] Cal. Veh. Code §§ 12800-12805.

[394] *Id.*

[395] *See, e.g.,* Uniform Veh. Code § 6-112.

[396] *See* GM, *GM 363 Asset Sale Approved by U.S. Bankruptcy Court,* July 6, 2009, publish.media.gm.com/content/media/us/en/news/news_detail.brand _gm.html/content/Pages/news/us/en/2009/Jul/0706_AssetSale ("[The court] approved the sale of substantially all of General Motors Corporation's assets to NGMCO, Inc., an entity funded by the U.S. Department of the Treasury. In connection with the closing of the sale transaction, NGMCO, Inc. will change its name to General Motors Company and continue to operate under GM's historic corporate and sub brands.").

[397] *See* Google, *Google's mission is to organize the world's information and make it universally accessible and useful,* www.google.com/intl/en/about/company/. In some states, Google might be allowed to drive itself to school. *See, e.g.,* Nev. Rev. Stat. § 483.270; Nev. Admin. Code § 483.200.

[398] Note, however, that certain requirements are statutory and hence binding on the relevant state agency. *See, e.g.,* Cal. Veh. Code § 12805 (specifying "[m]andatory grounds" for a "[r]efusal to issue or renew driver's license" and providing that "[n]o person may use a bioptic telescopic or similar lens to meet the 20/200 visual acuity standards").

[399] These arguments have been made, largely unsuccessfully, by persons with low vision who wish to use bioptic telescopics to pass a driver's license examination. *See, e.g., Hatch v. Sec'y of State of*

Maine, 879 F. Supp. 147, 148 (D. Maine 1995); *Gooch v. Iowa Dept. of Transp.*, 398 N.W.2d 845, 845 (Iowa 1987); *Sharon v. Larson*, 650 F. Supp. 1396, 1397 (E.D. Pa. 1986); *cf. Theriault v. Flynn*, 162 F.3d 46, 47-48 (1st Cir. 1998).

400 *See, e.g.*, Uniform Veh. Code §§ 1-192, 1-209.

401 *E.g., id.* § 11-106; 75 Pa. Cons. Stat. § 3706; R.I. Gen. Laws § 31-22-19.

402 *See generally* Joseph Bassano et al., *Motor vehicle—Trailer or semitrailer*, 60 C.J.S. Motor Vehicles § 3 ("A trailer or semitrailer is generally recognized as being a vehicle, and depending on the particular facts and circumstances, it may, or may not, be considered to be a motor vehicle. Insofar as it facilitates the primary function of a motor vehicle of transporting persons and things, after being attached to the motor vehicle for that purpose, it may be regarded as becoming a part of the motor vehicle although as to the latter proposition, there is also authority to the contrary.") (internal footnotes omitted); *see also, e.g.*, N.C. Gen. Stat. § 20-4.01(23) (including within the definition of "motor vehicle" "every vehicle designed to run upon the highways which is pulled by a self-propelled vehicle"); Wis. Stat. § 340.01(35) (including "a combination of 2 or more vehicles or an articulated vehicle"); *supra* note 304 (listing multiple definitions of driver referring to "steering a vehicle being towed by a motor vehicle"); *cf. also* 49 C.F.R. § 387.15 (defining motor vehicle as "a land vehicle, machine, truck, tractor, trailer, or semitrailer propelled or drawn by mechanical power and used on a highway for transporting property, or any combination thereof").

403 *E.g.*, Uniform Veh. Code § 1-156; Cal. Veh. Code § 415(a).

404 *Cf. also supra* note 14. And thanks for reading the footnotes.

405 Cal. Veh. Code § 22515.

406 *E.g.*, Tex. Transp. Code § 545.404; 75 Pa. Cons. Stat. § 3701.

407 *E.g.*, N.Y. Veh. & Traf. Law § 1210; Mass. Gen. Laws ch. 90, § 13.

408 Navajo Nation Code tit. 14, § 533.

409 *See, e.g., Car In Reverse Ghost Riding Out Of Control Doing Donuts For 7 Mins!*, www.youtube.com/watch?v=sZ0ICmr7W88 (not to be attempted at home). An astute reader might wonder at what point the man who jumped in the car became its driver.

410 Wash. Rev. Code § 46.61.590.

[411] 625 Ill. Comp. Stat. 5/11-1302.

[412] Ga. Code § 40-11-3.1.

[413] *E.g.*, 75 Pa. Cons. Stat. § 3744. Furthermore, would another driver involved in a crash with an unoccupied automated vehicle be expected to simply attach a note to its windshield? *See, e.g.*, Fla. Stat. § 316.063.

[414] *E.g.*, Ala. Code § 32-5A-151.

[415] Ohio Rev. Code § 4513.263.

[416] *See supra* part 6.1.1.

[417] Ohio Rev. Code § 4513.23.

[418] Wash. Rev. Code § 46.37.400.

[419] *E.g.*, Cal. Veh. Code § 21700; Tex. Transp. Code § 545.417; Mich. Comp. Laws § 257.677; Ga. Code § 40-6-242; Wash. Rev. Code § 46.61.615; Ind. Code § 9-21-8-43. Sight is mentioned in other provisions as well. *E.g.*, Tex. Transp. Code § 544.010(c) ("In the absence of a stop line, the operator shall stop at the place nearest the intersecting roadway where the operator has a view of approaching traffic on the intersecting roadway."); Ohio Rev. Code § 4513.24 (permitting certain electronic devices provided that, inter alia, they do "not restrict the vehicle operator's sight lines to the road and highway signs and signals").

[420] *See supra* part 6.1.1.

[421] *Id.*

[422] N.Y. Veh. & Traf. Law § 375.

[423] *Id.* § 1226

[424] Mass. Gen. Laws ch. 90, § 13.

[425] P.R. Laws tit. 27, § 5296. A separate provision, directed at motor vehicles, specifies that "[n]o person shall drive a motor vehicle on the public roads with persons, animals or objects obstructing the visibility of the driver towards the front or the sides of the vehicle or that interfere with the control of the driving mechanism of the vehicle." *Id.* § 5288.

[426] *See, e.g.*, Nat'l Highway Transp. Safety Bd., *Accident Report, Multivehicle Collision, Interstate 44 Eastbound, Gray Summit, Missouri, August 5, 2010*, NTSB/HAR-11/03, PB2011-916203 (Dec. 13, 2011), www.ntsb.gov/doclib/reports/2011/HAR1103.pdf.

[427] Mich. Comp. Laws § 257.326; *see also* Uniform Veh. Code § 16-102 ("Offenses by persons owning or controlling vehicles"); Cal. Veh. Code § 22515(a) ("No person driving, or in control of, or in charge of, a motor vehicle shall permit it to stand on any highway unattended without first effectively setting the brakes thereon and stopping the motor thereof."); 625 Ill. Comp. Stat. 5/11-203 ("No person shall wilfully fail or refuse to comply with any lawful order or direction of any police officer, fireman, or school crossing guard invested by law with authority to direct, control, or regulate traffic."); 75 Pa. Cons. Stat. § 3102 (same); Mich. Comp. Laws § 257.602 ("A person shall not refuse to comply with a lawful order or direction of a police officer when that officer, for public interest and safety, is guiding, directing, controlling, or regulating traffic on the highways of this state."); *see also* Fla. Stat. § 316.56 ("Such damage may be recovered in any civil action brought by the authorities in control of the highway or highway structure."); Ohio Rev. Code § 4511.203 ("No person shall permit a motor vehicle owned by the person or under the person's control to be driven by another if any of the following apply...."); Mass. Gen. Laws ch. 90, § 12(b) ("Whoever knowingly permits a motor vehicle owned by him or under his control to be operated by a person who is unlicensed or whose license has been suspended or revoked shall be punished...."); Wis. Stat. §§ 346.175 ("...if the person operating the vehicle or having the vehicle under his or her control at the time of the violation..."), 346.945 (same); La. Rev. Stat. § 32:53 ("No person shall drive or move, nor cause or knowingly permit any vehicle owned or controlled by him to be driven or moved, on any highway of this state, at any time, any [unsafe] vehicle...."); Ark. Code § 27-16-304 ("No person shall authorize or knowingly permit a motor vehicle owned by him or her or under his or her control to be driven upon any highway by any person who is not authorized under this chapter or is in violation of any of the provisions of this act."); W. Va. Code § 17B-4-4 ("No person shall authorize or knowingly permit a motor vehicle owned by him or under his control to be driven upon any highway by any person who is not authorized hereunder or in violation of any of the provisions of this chapter."); Neb. Rev. Stat. § 60-6,168 ("No person having control or charge of a motor vehicle shall allow such vehicle to stand unattended on a highway without first stopping the motor of such vehicle, locking the ignition, removing the key from the ignition, and effectively setting the brakes thereon and, when standing upon any roadway, turning the front wheels of such vehicle to the curb or side of such roadway."); Del. Code tit. 21, § 4172A ("No owner or person in charge of a motor vehicle shall permit that motor vehicle or any motor vehicle under the person's control to be operated by another person in such a manner as to cause wilful, wanton or reckless damage to or destruction of property

owned by another person, party, company or corporation, nor so as to cause or threaten to cause injury or death to any person.").

[428] Tex. Transp. Code § 545.304. Texas, among other states, also refers to "control" of a vehicle's speed. *E.g.*, *id.* § 545.351; Fla. Stat. § 316.183; Wash. Rev. Code § 46.61.400.

[429] N.J. Stat. § 39:4-53; *see also* Conn. Gen. Stat. § 14-228.

[430] N.C. Gen. Stat. § 20-123.1.

[431] Ohio Rev. Code § 4511.202.

[432] *See supra* part 4.

[433] See *infra* part 6.3.3 for a discussion of what standard might apply.

[434] *See supra* 4.4.1.

[435] This obligation might also be, and in some cases is, called a duty of care, but this term has a somewhat different meaning in tort law. The term "prudence" regularly appears in the "basic speed law," *e.g.*, *Wilding*, 156 Cal.App.2d at 379, which in its common formulation holds that "[n]o person shall drive ... at a speed greater than is reasonable and prudent under the conditions and having regard to the actual and potential hazards then existing," *e.g.*, Fla. Stat. § 316.183(1). In contrast, the German traffic code (Strassenverkehrsordnung (StVO)) specifies that "der Fahrzeugführer darf nur so schnell fahren, daß er sein Fahrzeug ständig beherrscht" (the driver may travel only as fast as he can while constantly controlling his vehicle). 3 Abs. 1 S. 1 StVO.

[436] *E.g.*, Fla. Stat. § 316.192.

[437] *State v. Conyers*, 506 N.W.2d 442, 444 (Iowa 1993).

[438] *Id.* at 445. *But see People v. Friesen*, 374 N.E.2d 15, 19 (Ill. App. Ct. 1978) (driver who killed a pedestrian while driving with only parking lights was negligent but not criminally negligent). More generally, as one Illinois court explained, "[r]eckless driving cases appear to fall into three general categories." *People v. Paarlberg*, 612 N.E.2d 106, 110 (1993). In the first, the driver commits multiple traffic offenses, such as speeding and weaving, that collectively demonstrate her culpability. *Id.* In the second, the driver consciously and egregiously disregards "particular surroundings and circumstances" by, for example, deliberately forcing a pedestrian off the road. *Id.* at 110-11. And in the third, the "willful and wanton conduct is based, in part, upon the driver's intoxication or impaired state." *Id.* at 111.

[439] Va. Code § 46.2-853. In addition, "[a] person shall be guilty of reckless driving who drives a motor vehicle on the highways in the Commonwealth (i) at a speed of twenty miles per hour or more in excess of the applicable maximum speed limit or (ii) in excess of eighty miles per hour regardless of the applicable maximum speed limit." *Id.* § 46.2-862. This second prong means that a person driving 81 mph on a Virginia freeway that is signed for 70 mph is driving recklessly—and could lose her DC license as long as reckless driving in Virginia and reckless driving in the District of Columbia are treated as equivalent offenses. Mike DeBonis, *D.C. drivers hurt by tough interpretation of Va. Offenses*, Wash. Post, July 30, 2012, www.washingtonpost.com/local/dc-politics/dc-drivers-hurt-by-tough-interpretation-of-va-offenses/2012/07/30/gJQAzPbBLX_story.html; Mike DeBonis, *D.C. Council fixes DMV's reckless driving lunacy*, Wash. Post, September 19, 2012, www.washingtonpost.com/blogs/mike-debonis/post/dc-council-fixes-dmvs-reckless-driving-lunacy/2012/09/19/6bb5ceca-0291-11e2-8102-ebee9c66e190_blog.html.

[440] Fla. Stat. § 316.1925; La. Rev. Stat. § 32:58.

[441] N.J. Stat. § 39:4-97.2.

[442] *Id.* § 39:4-97.

[443] Haw. Rev. Stat. § 291-12.

[444] Wyo. Stat. § 31-5-236.

[445] N.Y. Veh. & Traf. Law § 1146; *accord* Uniform Veh. Code § 11-504; Ariz. Rev. Stat. § 28-794; Tenn. Code § 55-8-136; Mo. Rev. Stat. § 300.410; La. Rev. Stat. § 32:214; Miss. Code § 63-3-1112; Kan. Stat. § 8-1535.

[446] Okla. Stat. tit. 47, § 11-901b.

[447] *Id.*

[448] *See* Tenn. Code § 55-8-136 ("Notwithstanding any speed limit or zone in effect at the time, or right-of-way rules that may be applicable, every driver of a vehicle shall exercise due care by operating the vehicle at a safe speed, by maintaining a safe lookout, by keeping the vehicle under proper control and by devoting full time and attention to operating the vehicle, under the existing circumstances as necessary in order to be able to see and to avoid endangering life, limb or property and to see and avoid colliding with any other vehicle or person, or any road sign, guard rail or any fixed object either legally using or legally parked or legally placed, upon any roadway, within or beside the roadway right-of-way including, but

not limited to, any adjacent sidewalk, bicycle lane, shoulder or berm.").

[449] Ga. Code § 40-6-241. However, "the proper use of a radio, citizens band radio, mobile telephone, or amateur or ham radio shall not be a violation of this Code section." *Id.*

[450] Wis. Stat. § 346.89.

[451] Ark. Code § 27-51-104.

[452] Me. Rev. Stat. tit. 29-a, § 2118. Notably, the statute does not specify that the driver be at fault in the crash. *Id.*

[453] D.C. Code § 50-1731.03.

[454] *Id.* § 50-1731.02(1).

[455] *E.g.*, Governors Highway Safety Association, *Cell Phone and Texting Laws, October 2012,* www.ghsa.org/html/stateinfo/laws/cellphone_laws.html; Uniform Veh. Code §§ 11-104, 12-410; N.Y. Veh. & Traf. Law §§ 1225-c, 1225-d, 1229-c.

[456] Or. Rev. Stat. § 811.190; Wash. Rev. Code § 46.61.665. Alaska has not been concerned since 1979. *See* 13 AAC § 02.540 ("Embracing another while driving") (repealed June 28, 1979).

[457] N.J. Stat. § 2C:11-5(a) ("Proof that the defendant fell asleep while driving or was driving after having been without sleep for a period in excess of 24 consecutive hours may give rise to an inference that the defendant was driving recklessly."); *see generally* Joshua D. Levine, *A Road to Injustice Paved with Good Intentions: Maggie's Misguided Crackdown on Drowsy Driving*, 56 Hastings L.J. 1297 (2005); *cf. also* Tasmania Law Reform Institute, *Criminal Liability of Drivers Who Fall Asleep Causing Motor Vehicle Crashes Resulting in Death or Other Serious Injury:* Jiminez, Final Report No. 13, October 2010, www.law.utas.edu.au/reform/documents/JiminezA4.pdf.

[458] *See, e.g., Friesen*, 374 N.E.2d at 19.

[459] *See* Robert F. Koets, William Lindsley, Sarah Newcomb, and Susan L. Thomas, *What amounts to reckless driving of motor vehicle within statute making such a criminal offense*, 52 A.L.R.2d 1337; Cal. Veh. Code ch. 12 (penalizing reckless driving and particular acts that may be negligent, but not categorically penalizing negligent driving); Cal. Penal Code § 192(c)(2)) (defining one type of vehicular manslaughter as "the unlawful killing of a human being without malice" while "driving a vehicle in the commission of a lawful

act which might produce death, in an unlawful manner, but without gross negligence"); *People v. Bussel*, 118 Cal. Rptr. 2d 159, 163 (Cal. App. 2002) (discussing Cal. Penal Code § 192(c)(2)). Drivers who kill or seriously injure pedestrians and cyclists without serious consequence provide particularly tragic examples of the inadequacy and underenforcement of existing vehicle laws. *See, e.g.*, Jason R. Holmes, *Share the Road: Why the Current Laws in Arizona Do Not Adequately Protect Cyclists, and A Call to Legislators to Change Those Laws*, 5 Phoenix L. Rev. 591 (2012); Alex Goldmark, *Killed While Cycling: Why So Few Fatal Bike Crashes Lead to Arrest in NYC*, transportationnation.org/2012/04/08/killed-while-cycling-why-so-few-fatal-bike-crashes-lead-to-arrest-in-nyc; Brad Aaron, *Is There Really a "Rule of Two"?*, www.streetsblog.org/2012/02/22/is-there-really-a-rule-of-two; Transportation Alternatives, *Deadly Driving Unlimited: How the NYPD Lets Drivers Run Wild*, www.transalt.org/files/newsroom/reports/2012/Deadly_Driving_Unlim ited_Report.pdf; Samantha Shimogawa, *Kill a Cyclist and Get Away With It?*, www.bicyclepaper.com/articles/389-Kill-a-Cyclist-and-Get-Away-With-It-.

[460] *See* Joseph Bassano, et al., 60A C.J.S. Motor Vehicles § 587 ("The duty to operate a motor vehicle with due and reasonable care and caution under the circumstances exists at common law and is not dependent on any statutory requirements.").

[461] *Compare, e.g.*, *Berlin v. Violett*, 129 Cal. App. 337, 340-41 (1933) ("Appellant objects to the giving immediately thereafter of the following instruction: 'All drivers of vehicles on a public highway are required by law to keep a vigilant lookout ahead so as to avoid, if reasonably possible, a collision with any other vehicle or person lawfully upon such highway. Failure to keep such lookout, or failure to see that which may be readily seen, if the driver is looking, would constitute negligence as a matter of law.' We find no error in this instruction.") *with Fielder v. Magnolia Beverage Co.*, 757 So. 2d 925, 935 (Miss. 1999) ("[T]his Court has held that instructions which require vigilance on the part of a driver [are to be] condemned as requiring more than the exercise of reasonable care on the part of a motorist. *See Turner v. Turner*, 524 So.2d 942, 947 (Miss.1988) (holding an instruction erroneous because it placed a higher burden on the driver Turner than that of reasonable care); Crossley v. James, 365 So.2d 957 (Miss.1978) (holding that it was reversible error to grant an instruction which places upon defendant the burden of avoiding a collision); *Jones v. Phillips*, 263 So.2d 759, 762-63 (Miss.1972) ('avoid the collision' and 'vigilant lookout' instructions were erroneous, because both instructions, considered together, placed a higher duty upon defendant than the law requires). *But see*

Miles v. Duckworth, 481 So.2d 757, 758 (Miss.1985) (upheld an instruction that stated that if defendant 'failed to keep a reasonable and proper lookout for other traffic and vehicles; or if he failed to have his vehicle under reasonable and proper control .... then such action or actions, if any, ... constitutes negligence').").

[462] *See generally* James Buchwalter et al., 8 Am. Jur. 2d Automobiles §§ 420-22; Joseph Bassano, 60A C.J.S. Motor Vehicles §§ 662-67.

[463] *Warren v. Bostock*, 170 Neb. 203, 207-08, 102 N.W.2d 55, 58 (Neb. 1960).

[464] *Hodder v. United States*, 328 F. Supp. 2d 335, 341 (E.D.N.Y. 2004) (citing New York cases to characterize New York law) (internal citations omitted).

[465] *Jones v. Schabron*, 2005 WY 65, 113 P.3d 34, 38 (Wyo. 2005) (quotation omitted).

[466] *Pike Taxi Co. v. Patterson*, 258 Ala. 508, 511, 63 So. 2d 599, 602 (Ala. 1952) (quotation omitted).

[467] This conclusion describes not only motor vehicles generally but specific contemporary features like cruise control.

[468] This could also be described in terms of omission: The driver fails to prevent this poor performance.

[469] This also applies to civil negligence in the case of a crash that vigilance would have prevented. The driver is negligent if her duty of vigilance is absolute, but she might not be negligent if her duty is contextual and her reliance on her vehicle was reasonable. The underlying common law duty can vary by environment but not by driver. *See* Joseph Bassano, et al., 60A C.J.S. Motor Vehicles § 584 ("Notwithstanding that the degree of diligence or attention required to constitute due care may vary with the circumstances, the legal standard of care required is unvarying and alike at all times and, in the absence of a statute providing otherwise, applies equally to all, regardless of age, sex, experience, or mental or physical ability."). Skeptical judges and juries may conceivably treat automated vehicles (and their drivers) differently than conventional vehicles (and their drivers), and, to the extent that mere presence of an automated vehicle on the highway is the cause of an injury, the doctrine of inherently dangerous products may arguably supply a legal basis for that difference. *Cf. generally* Joseph Bassano, et al., 60 C.J.S. Motor Vehicles § 22.

[470] Strassenverkehrsordnung (StVO).

[471] Gasser, *supra* note 34, at 13. The report notes concern that higher levels of automation could lead the driver to neglect these obligations. *Id.* at 14-16. However, it distinguishes (and condones) a vehicle's assumption of control if the driver becomes unexpectedly incapacitated. *Id.* at 16-17.

[472] *See supra* note 455.

[473] *See supra* part 6.2; *infra* part 6.3.3.

[474] *See supra* note 469.

[475] Tex. Transp. Code § 545.002.

[476] *See infra* parts 6.3.1-6.3.2.

[477] *See infra* part 6.3.3.

[478] States may also impose particular requirements on motor vehicle manufacturers. *See, e.g.,* Uniform Veh. Code § 12-106 (proof of compliance with standards); 625 Ill. Comp. Stat. 5/5-109; Conn. Gen. Stat. § 14-67a (registration). The definition of manufacturer may be particularly relevant to any person retrofitting a conventional motor vehicle with automation technology.

[479] In general, a "vehicle" is "[e]very device in, upon, or by which any person or property is *or may be* transported or drawn upon a highway, excepting devices used exclusively upon stationary rails or tracks." Uniform Veh. Code § 1-215 (emphasis added). A "motor vehicle" is "[e]very vehicle which is self-propelled, and every vehicle which is propelled by electric power obtained from overhead trolley wires but not operated upon rails, except vehicles moved solely by human power and motorized wheelchairs." *Id.* § 1-156.

[480] Many states also restrict "foreign" or "injurious" substances. *E.g.,* Fla. Stat. § 316.2044(1) ("Any person who drops, or permits to be dropped or thrown, upon any street or highway any destructive or injurious material shall immediately remove the same or cause it to be removed."); Wis. Stat. § 346.94(5) ("No person shall place or cause to be placed upon a highway any foreign substance which is or may be injurious to any vehicle or part thereof.").

[481] Cal. Veh. Code § 24002. The Uniform Vehicle Code extends this prohibition to owners: "It is a misdemeanor for any person to drive or move or for the owner to cause or knowingly permit to be driven or moved on any highway any vehicle or combination of vehicles which is in such unsafe condition as to endanger any person, or which [violates a vehicle equipment regulation]." Uniform Veh. Code § 12-101(a).

[482] Tex. Transp. Code § 547.004.

[483] Uniform Veh. Code § 13-102. California's provision is more formal: "Every driver of a passenger vehicle shall stop and submit the vehicle to an inspection of the mechanical condition and equipment of the vehicle at any location where members of the California Highway Patrol are conducting tests and inspections of passenger vehicles and when signs are displayed requiring such stop." Cal. Veh. Code § 2814.

[484] In California, for example, "[a] person shall not drive, move, or leave standing upon a highway, or in an offstreet public parking facility, any motor vehicle ... unless it is registered." Cal. Veh. Code § 4000(a)(1). An "offstreet public parking facility" is "[a]ny publicly owned parking facility" or "[a]ny privately owned parking facility for which no fee for the privilege to park is charged and which is held open for the common public use of retail customers," unless the vehicle is stored in that private facility "by, or with the express permission of," that facility's owner. *Id.* § 4000(a)(2).

[485] Cal. Veh. Code § 4751; *see also id.* § 24002 ("(a) It is unlawful to operate any vehicle or combination of vehicles which is in an unsafe condition, or which is not safely loaded, and which presents an immediate safety hazard. (b) It is unlawful to operate any vehicle or combination of vehicles which is not equipped as provided in this code.").

[486] N.Y. Veh. & Traf. Law § 400.

[487] Mass. Gen. Laws ch. 90, § 2.

[488] N.D. Cent. Code § 39-21-45.1.

[489] Cal. Veh. Code § 24008.

[490] 75 Pa. Cons. Stat. § 1165.1(b); Haw. Rev. Stat. § 286-85(a); Nev. Rev. Stat. § 482.223.

[491] Wis. Stat. § 341.268(e).

[492] R.I. Gen. Laws § 31-9-3.

[493] *See, e.g.*, 75 Pa. Cons. Stat. § 102 ("'Reconstructed vehicle.' A vehicle, other than an antique or classic vehicle, for which a certificate of salvage was issued and is thereafter restored to operating condition to meet the vehicle equipment and inspection standards under Part IV (relating to vehicle characteristics)"); Tenn. Code § 55-1-106(2) ("'Reconstructed vehicle' means every vehicle of a type required to be registered hereunder materially altered from its original construction by the removal, addition, or substitution of

essential parts, new or used...."); Wis. Stat. § 341.268(d) ("'Reconstructed vehicle' means a motor vehicle of any age which has been substantially altered or modified from original manufacturers specifications to such an extent that it no longer resembles the original manufactured vehicle."), (f) ("'Street modified vehicle" means a motor vehicle of any age which has been modified from original manufacturers specifications, but does not include any reconstructed vehicle as defined under par. (d)."); Or. Rev. Stat. § 801.408 ("'Reconstructed vehicle' means either: (1) A vehicle that: (a) Has a body that resembles and primarily is a particular year model or make of vehicle; (b) Is not a vehicle rebuilt by a manufacturer; (c) Is not a vehicle built in a factory where the year model and make are assigned at the factory; and (d) Is not a replica; or (2) A motor truck that has been rebuilt using a component kit if the manufacturer of the kit assigns a vehicle identification number and provides a manufacturer's certificate of origin for the kit."); Nev. Rev. Stat. § 482.100 ("'Reconstructed vehicle' means any vehicle which shall have been assembled or constructed largely by means of essential parts, new or used, derived from other vehicles or makes of vehicles of various names, models or types, or which, if originally otherwise constructed, shall have been materially altered by the removal of essential parts or by the addition or substitution of essential parts, new or used, derived from other vehicles or makes of vehicles."); Haw. Rev. Stat. § 286-2 ("'Reconstructed vehicle' means a vehicle that is registered to be operated on a public highway, and that is: (1) Assembled from new or used parts by a person other than a recognized manufacturer of new vehicles; (2) Modified to the extent that the identity of the vehicle's make, model, or type is obscured by material changes in its appearance; or (3) Modified by the removal, addition, alteration, or substitution of other than original replacement essential parts, including the vehicle's body, power train, steering system, suspension system, exhaust system, intake system, or bumper system; excluding ordinary body repair that does not change the exterior structure of the vehicle. The term does not include a special interest vehicle or a motorcycle."). "Essential parts" are generally "[a]ll integral and body parts ..., the removal, alteration, or substitution of which would tend to conceal the identity of the vehicle or substantially alter its appearance, model, type or mode of operation." Uniform. Veh. Code § 1-130. Theft and fraud are primary targets of the vehicle modification statutes. *See, e.g.,* 75 Pa. Cons. Stat. § 1165.1(b).

[494] *See supra* notes 417-418; *cf. also supra* note 112.

[495] Cal. Veh. Code § 24003.

[496] *Lamp*, Oxford English Dictionary ("A vessel containing oil, which is burnt at a wick, for the purpose of illumination. Now also a vessel of glass or some similar material, enclosing the source of illumination, whether a candle, oil, gas-jet, or incandescent wire.") (selected definition).

[497] *See, e.g.*, Velodyne, *High Definition Lidar HDL-64E S2*, www.velodynelidar.com/lidar/products/brochure/HDL-64E%20S2%20datasheet_2010_lowres.pdf (describing a class 1 laser with 905 nanometer wavelength in 5 nanosecond pulses).

[498] *See also supra* part 5.

[499] Mo. Rev. Stat. § 307.122.

[500] Ga. Code § 40-8-51(a).

[501] 49 U.S.C. § 30103(b)(1) ("When a [federal] motor vehicle safety standard is in effect ..., a State or a political subdivision of a State may prescribe or continue in effect a standard applicable to the same aspect of performance of a motor vehicle or motor vehicle equipment only if the standard is identical to the [federal] standard."); *see also* Uniform Veh. Code § 12-103 ("Where the U.S. Department of Transportation has issued a current Federal Motor Vehicle Safety Standard applicable to a particular item of vehicle equipment, a standard adopted by the [state's] department applicable to the same aspect shall of performance of that item of vehicle equipment shall be identical to the federal standard.").

[502] Cal. Veh. Code § 21461.

[503] *Id.* § 22350. This is often called the "basic speed law." *E.g., Wilding*, 156 Cal.App.2d at 379; *cf. also, e.g.*, Fla. Stat. §§ 316.183 ("(1) No person shall drive a vehicle on a highway at a speed greater than is reasonable and prudent under the conditions and having regard to the actual and potential hazards then existing. In every event, speed shall be controlled as may be necessary to avoid colliding with any person, vehicle, or other conveyance or object on or entering the highway in compliance with legal requirements and the duty of all persons to use due care.... (4) The driver of every vehicle shall, consistent with the requirements of subsection (1), drive at an appropriately reduced speed when: (a) Approaching and crossing an intersection or railway grade crossing; (b) Approaching and going around a curve; (c) Approaching a hill crest; (d) Traveling upon any narrow or winding roadway; and (e) Any special hazard exists with respect to pedestrians or other traffic or by reason of weather or highway conditions. (5) No person shall drive a motor vehicle at such a slow speed as to impede or block the normal and

reasonable movement of traffic, except when reduced speed is necessary for safe operation or in compliance with law."), 316.1925 ("Any person operating a vehicle upon the streets or highways within the state shall drive the same in a careful and prudent manner, having regard for the width, grade, curves, corners, traffic, and all other attendant circumstances, so as not to endanger the life, limb, or property of any person. Failure to drive in such manner shall constitute careless driving and a violation of this section.").

[504] Traveling above the posted speed limit is not necessarily unreasonable, and traveling below the posted speed limit is not necessarily reasonable.

[505] *See* Manual on Uniform Traffic Control Devices for Streets and Highways (MUTCD) (2009 ed.), § 2B.13 ("Guidance: ... When a speed limit within a speed zone is posted, it should be within 5 mph of the 85th-percentile speed of free-flowing traffic.").

[506] *Weaver v. Chavez*, 35 Cal.Rptr.3d 514, 133 Cal.App.4th 1350 (Cal. App. 2005).

[507] *Waxman v. Jennings*, 72 Cal. App. 671, 238 P. 98 (Cal. App. 1925).

[508] Cal. Veh. Code § 22400.

[509] *Id.* § 21950.

[510] *See, e.g.*, Douglas A. Kysar, *The Expectations of Consumers*, 103 Colum. L. Rev. 1700, 1763-66 (2003).

[511] *See, e.g.*, *People v. De Casaus* (Cal. App. 1957), 309 P.2d 835, *cert. denied*, 78 S.Ct. 262, 355 U.S. 890, 2 L.Ed.2d 189; *Ex parte Daniels* 183 Cal. 636 (Cal. 1920); *Garcia v. State*, 498 S.W.2d 936 (Tex. Crim. App. 1973). *But see, e.g., State v. Stanko*, 292 Mont. 192, 974 P.2d 1132 (Mont. 1998).

[512] At least those norms are written. Some community norms (such as waving a bicyclist through a stop sign) may be even more informal.

[513] *E.g.*, 75 Pa. Cons. Stat. § 3102 ("No person shall willfully fail or refuse to comply with any lawful order or direction of any uniformed police officer, sheriff or constable or, in an emergency, a railroad or street railway police officer; or any appropriately attired person, including an agent or employee of the funeral director during a funeral, authorized to direct, control or regulate traffic or an employee who has been trained in traffic control by a licensed and insured private security company and who is acting in the scope of employment."); Mich. Comp. Laws § 257.602 ("A person shall not

refuse to comply with a lawful order or direction of a police officer when that officer, for public interest and safety, is guiding, directing, controlling, or regulating traffic on the highways of this state."); Ga. Code § 40-6-2 ("No person shall fail or refuse to comply with any lawful order or direction of any police officer, firefighter, [authorized] police volunteer ..., or [authorized] school-crossing guard...."").

[514] *E.g.*, Va. Code § 46.2-834(B) ("Law-enforcement officers and uniformed school crossing guards may assume control of traffic otherwise controlled by lights, and in such event, signals by such officers and uniformed crossing guards shall take precedence over such traffic control devices.").

[515] *See supra* note 513.

[516] *See supra* part 3.

[517] *See infra* part 6.4.1.

[518] *See infra* part 6.4.2.

[519] *See infra* part 6.4.3.

[520] *See infra* part 6.4.4.

[521] *See supra* parts 6.2-6.3.

[522] "'Autonomous vehicle' means a motor vehicle that uses artificial intelligence, sensors and global positioning system coordinates to drive itself without the active intervention of a human operator." Nev. Rev. Stat. § 482A.030. "'Artificial intelligence' means the use of computers and related equipment to enable a machine to duplicate or mimic the behavior of human beings." *Id.* § 482A.020. "'Sensors' includes, without limitation, cameras, lasers and radar. *Id.* § 482A.050. "'Highway' means the entire width between the boundary lines of every way dedicated to a public authority when any part of the way is open to the use of the public for purposes of vehicular traffic, whether or not the public authority is maintaining the way." *Id.* § 484A.095.

[523] *Id.* § 482A.100.

[524] *Id.*

[525] *Cf. id.* § 483.270; Nev. Admin. Code § 483.200.

[526] Nev. Rev. Stat. § 484B.165 par. 7.

[527] *See infra* note 567.

[528] Nevada DMV, *Adopted Regulation of the Department of Motor Vehicles*, LCB File No. R084-11, Effective March 1, 2012,

www.leg.state.nv.us/register/RegsReviewed/$R084-11_ADOPTED.pdf, § 2.

[529] Nevada DMV, *Informational Statement of Adopted Regulations as Required by Administrative Procedures Act*, NRS 233B.066, LCB File No. R084-11, February 6, 2012, www.leg.state.nv.us/register/RegsReviewed/$R084-11_Statement.pdf, at 3.

[530] *Adopted Regulation, supra* note 528, § 2.

[531] Consider, for example, a vehicle that can drive itself on freeways but not on city streets or that can operate in certain conditions without the "active control or continuous monitoring of a natural person" but that nonetheless requires a human to assume control shortly after a takeover request. *Cf., e.g.*, Continental, *Continental tests highly-automated driving* (March 23, 2012), www.conti-online.com/generator/www/com/en/continental/pressportal/themes/press_releases/3_automotive_group/chassis_safety/press_releases/pr_2012_03_23_automated_driving_en,version=2.html ("More than 6,000 miles of highly-automated driving on public roads in Nevada were completed and had the aim to show that it becomes possible to develop room for freedom for the driver which does not serve primary vehicle guidance and therefore provide the driver a welcome change in certain situations."); Audi USA, *Driver assistance systems* (January 10, 2012), www.audiusanews.com/newsrelease.do;jsessionid=303EC9E15BF1151465A9815C2ED2EC38?&id=2757 ("The traffic jam assistant … can relieve the driver at times when driving is not much fun, such as in congested traffic. At speeds between zero and 60 km/h (37.28 mph), the system helps to steer the car within certain constraints. It also accelerates and brakes autonomously. The traffic jam assistant can be used on expressways or in cities, provided that the course of the road is not too complex.").

[532] *See infra* parts 6.4.2, 6.4.3, 6.4.4.

[533] *Adopted Regulation, supra* note 528, §§ 3-4.

[534] *See supra* part 6.2; *see also* Sarah Jacobsson Purewal, *Nevada Approves Self-Driving Cars after Google Lobbying Push*, PCWorld, Feb. 17, 2012, www.pcworld.com/article/250179/nevada_approves_self_driving_cars_after_google_lobbying_push.html,

("According to [DMV director Bruce] Breslow, operators of driverless cars will be allowed to text and drive – but not drink and drive. 'There is no exemption for drinking and driving,' he told the AP.").

[535] *Informational Statement*, *supra* note 529, at 6; *see also* DMV, *Autonomous Vehicles*, www.dmvnv.com/autonomous.htm ("Currently, the DMV is accepting applications for testing only. Autonomous vehicles are not available to the general public.").

[536] *Compare Adopted Regulation*, *supra* note 528, § 8 *with id.* § 16.

[537] *Adopted Regulation*, *supra* note 528, §§ 8, 16.

[538] *Id.* § 8.

[539] *Id.* § 16.

[540] *See* Nevada DMV, *Autonomous Vehicle Testing License*, OBL326 (January 2012), www.dmvnv.com/pdfforms/obl326.pdf.

[541] $1 million for up to 5 vehicles, $2 million for 6 to 10 vehicles, and $3 million for more than 10 vehicles. *Adopted Regulation*, *supra* note 528,§ 8.

[542] *Id.* §§ 8-11.

[543] *Id.* § 12.

[544] *Id.* § 9.

[545] A portion of urban Las Vegas is currently Nevada's only "complex urban environment." *Autonomous Vehicle Testing License*, *supra* note 540.

[546] *Id.*

[547] *Adopted Regulation*, *supra* note 528, § 10.

[548] *Id.*

[549] *Id.* §§ 4, 16.

[550] *Id.* § 5.

[551] *Id.* §§ 6, 16.

[552] *Id.* § 16.

[553] *See id.* § 6.

[554] *Id.* § 16.

[555] *Id.* § 18.

[556] *Id.* § 19.

[557] *Id.* § 6.

[558] *Id.* § 23.

559 *Id.* §§ 5, 27.

560 *See id.* §§ 5, 10.

561 *Id.* § 5.

562 *Id.* § 6.

563 *Id.*

564 Fla. CS/HB 1207 (2012), *codified in* Fla. Stat. chs. 316, 319.

565 Fla. CS/HB 1207 §§ 1, 2, *codified in* Fla. Stat. § 316.003.

566 Fla. CS/HB 1207 § 1.

567 Curiously, the legislative analysis of CS/HB 1207 contradicts this finding by asserting that "[t]he only jurisdiction in the world where it is legal to operate autonomous vehicles on public roads is in the state of Nevada, where a law authorizing them passed in June 2011." House of Representatives, *Final Bill Analysis, CS/HB 1207, Summary   Analysis,* www.myfloridahouse.gov/Sections/Documents/loaddoc.aspx?FileNa me=h1207z1.THSS.DOCX& DocumentType=Analysis&BillNumber=1207&Session=2012, at 2.

568 Fla. CS/HB 1207 (2012) § 3, *codified in* Fla. Stat. § 316.85.

569 Fla. CS/HB 1207 (2012) § 3, *codified in* Fla. Stat. § 316.85.

570 The vehicle must "continue to meet federal standards and regulations for a motor vehicle," have an "easily accessible" "means to engage and disengage the autonomous technology," provide a visual indication inside the vehicle that "the vehicle is operating in autonomous mode," provide an alert of a "technology failure affecting the ability of the vehicle to safely operate autonomously," and "[b]e capable of being operated in compliance with the applicable traffic and motor vehicle laws of this state." Fla. CS/HB 1207 (2012) § 4, *codified in* Fla. Stat. § 319.145. NHTSA regulations "shall supersede" these requirements "when found to be in conflict with" them. *Id.*

571 A human operator able "to monitor ... and intervene" must be present in the vehicle if tested in traffic, and "the entity performing the testing must submit [a satisfactory] instrument of insurance, surety bond, or proof of self-insurance ... in the amount of $5 million." Fla. CS/HB 1207 (2012) § 5, *codified in* Fla. Stat. § 319.145.

572 Fla. CS/HB 1207 (2012) § 5, *codified in* Fla. Stat. § 316.86. Neither the legislation nor Florida's motor vehicle statutes defines the

term "original manufacturer." *See* Fla. CS/HB 1207; Fla. Stat. chs. 316-25.

[573] Cal. SB 1298 (2012), *codified in* Cal. Vehicle Code div. 16.6 (§ 38750).

[574] Cal. SB 1298 § 1.

[575] *Id.*

[576] *Id.* § 2.

[577] *Id.*

[578] *Id.*

[579] *Id.*

[580] *Id.*

[581] *Id.*

[582] *Id.*

[583] *Id.*

[584] Bryant Walker Smith, *Automated Driving: Legislative and Regulatory Action*, cyberlaw.stanford.edu/wiki/index.php/Automated_Driving:_Legislativ e_and_Regulatory_Action.

[585] Bryant Walker Smith, *Automated Driving: State Model Bill*, cyberlaw.stanford.edu/wiki/index.php/Automated_Driving:_State_Mo del_Bill.

[586] *See infra* §§ 3.7-3.9, 5, 7.3.

[587] This language provides a legislative basis for courts and administrative agencies to more flexibly interpret existing and new law with respect to automated vehicles.

[588] This provision expressly preserves existing interpretations of driving laws as applied to conventional vehicles and automated vehicles being operated conventionally. The "transitioning" language is necessary to cover cases where automated operation has ended but no human has resumed real-time input or where a platoon is dispersing. *See infra* §§ 3.7-3.9, 7.6. Some new provisions in this draft, however, do apply to both conventional and automated vehicles. *See, e.g., infra* §§ 4, 7.8, 7.9.

[589] This language ensures that state statutes regarding owner liability (for the purpose of, inter alia, insurance, moving and parking violations, and driver negligence) are not affected by changes to,

inter alia, the definition of driver and the rules of the road. *See supra* part 6.1.3; *infra* §§ 3.7-3.9, 7. For example, even if the vehicle owner does not directly initiate automated operation, the vehicle's effective driver would still be considered a permitted driver for the purpose of vicarious civil liability. However, this language does not preclude specification of minimum levels of *criminal* culpability. *See infra* §§ 7.9-7.10.

[590] *See supra* part 4.5.4.

[591] *See infra* § 3.5.

[592] *See infra* §§ 3.11-3.12.

[593] *See infra* § 5.

[594] *See infra* § 5.

[595] This language covers privacy and security of and access to data, including logs for crashes and other incidents.

[596] This provision gives the Department the authority, but not the obligation, to enact rules other than those specifically mandated in this section. This is because an extensive ex ante rulemaking process may be futile, wasteful, or limiting when many questions of implementation, including the proper treatment of particular technologies and products, are likely to be highly novel or contextual.

[597] This language recognizes (and perhaps invites) federal preemption. *See supra* part 5. It also encourages other means of standardization. SAE International has an autonomous vehicle standards committee (on which I serve). *See supra* note 38. California is the most populous state and may be one of the first to promulgate automated vehicle performance standards. *See supra* part 6.4.3.

[598] Vehicle automation implicates issues and expertise that may lie outside a department of motor vehicles. The names and organizational relationships of agencies vary by state.

[599] Florida's autonomous driving statute requires such a report. *See supra* part 6.4.2.

[600] *See supra* part 3. This definition may be broader than those adopted to date. *See supra* part 6.4. However, the Department may define multiple automation profiles. *See supra* § 3.5; *infra* § 6.3.

[601] *Id.* Accordingly, an automated vehicle is not necessarily under automated operation.

[602] The Nevada, Florida, and California laws use the term "autonomous technology" to refer to a similar concept. *See supra* part 6.4. The concept is particularly relevant to the conversion of a conventional production vehicle into an automated vehicle. *See infra* § 4.2.

[603] *See infra* §§ 3.7-3.9. The transition from automated operation raises difficult questions regarding responsibility. Even if automated operation has terminated, the effective driver's responsibility continues until an ordinary human driver has actually intervened. This language also balances, no doubt imperfectly, the risk of a human intervening when inappropriate with the risk of a human failing to intervene when needed.

[604] This refers to the relevant characteristics of the vehicle, human, and environment, including the level of automation and the domain of operation. *See supra* part 3.

[605] Agency names and responsibilities vary by state. *See also supra* note 598.

[606] *See supra* § 3.4; *supra* text accompanying note 586.

[607] *Id.* Depending on the jurisdiction, the modifier "exclusive" may be too restrictive. *Cf., e.g., supra* note 305.

[608] This provision specifies that the ordinary human driver remains responsible if an emergency intervention system engages automatically because of an impending crash or because that driver has become incapacitated.

[609] This applies only if the vehicle actually has a virtual driver. *See infra* §§ 3.13, 5.2.

[610] If there is no virtual driver, then the person who initiated automated operation is the effective driver. This is similar to Nevada and Florida law. *See supra* parts 6.4.1, 6.4.2. The Department may establish a presumption that another person, such as the vehicle occupant nearest the conventional apparatus, has initiated automated operation. *Cf. supra* part 6.4.3 (California driver rule for autonomous vehicles); *supra* note 362 (Wisconsin driver presumptions).

[611] This applies if no natural person initiates automated operation, which could conceivably occur with automated taxi dispatch, carsharing fleet management, fully automated delivery, and other advanced logistics applications.

[612] This language potentially broadens the criminal and civil liability of a person who causes or could cause harm with an automated vehicle but who may not otherwise be considered a driver.

[613] *See* Uniform Veh. Code § 1-152; *infra* § 5.2.3. This definition excludes a person who only manufacturers or installs an automation package.

[614] *See supra* § 2.2.

[615] This refers to the relevant characteristics of the vehicle, human, and environment, including the level of automation and the domain of operation. *See supra* part 3.

[616] *See supra* § 3.9; *infra* § 5.2. This language leaves open the possibility that, for example, a vehicle may have a virtual driver during automated parking but not during highway cruising.

[617] This provision enables the Department to identify the technical capability of every vehicle registered in the state. Current vehicle identification numbers (VINs), for example, do not indicate whether vehicles have any driver assistance systems. *See supra* note 265. The provision also links certain vehicles with virtual drivers. *See infra* § 5.2.

[618] The vehicle registration process can provide a mechanism for supervising the safety of automated vehicles, including aftermarket conversions of conventional vehicles. If an automation package is installed, customized, or changed on a vehicle, the owner of that vehicle must reregister it. Voluntary and involuntary recalls, manufacturer upgrades, and changes to certain test vehicles are exempted. In addition, the Department can promulgate rules that provide flexibility in the application or administration of this provision.

[619] *See id.* This provision enables the Department to indirectly prohibit (albeit not prevent) the operation of any vehicle that it determines to be unsafe, provided that the vehicle is registered in the state. This provision complements the direct prohibition on such operation, which also applies to out-of-state vehicles. *See infra* § 7.8.

[620] This is intended to facilitate standardization and reduce the workload on the Department. *See also supra* § 2.7.

[621] This specifies that no court should deem a vehicle to be safe or lawful simply because it is registered.

[622] This draft maintains the requirement that drivers be licensed and therefore enables certain persons who are currently ineligible for a license to receive a conditional license valid only for automated vehicles with certain characteristics, regardless of whether such

vehicles yet exist. *See supra* part 6.2.1. Operation may involve simply starting a vehicle and initiating automated operation. *See supra* § 3.9.

[623] *See supra* text accompanying note 586.

[624] Requirements might address, inter alia, the performance of the automated vehicles and the ability of the applicant or its insurer to pay any judgments entered against it. *See also infra* note 626.

[625] Again, this language leaves open the possibility that, for example, a vehicle may have a virtual driver during automated parking but not during highway cruising. *See supra* note 616.

[626] This language expressly permits but does not require the Department to restrict virtual licenses to entities that are already subject to well-established regulatory regimes and that have a connection to the vehicles covered. Such a requirement may also ensure that virtual licenses are not used to limit liability exposure. *Cf., e.g., Walkovsky v. Carlton*, 223 N.E.2d 6 (N.Y. 1966).

[627] *See, e.g., supra* notes 395-397.

[628] *Cf. supra* § 4.3.

[629] *Cf. supra* § 1.1.

[630] *See supra* § 4.3; *infra* § 7.8. This provision also applies to vehicles registered outside the state.

[631] This draft does not address specific substantive safety standards for automated vehicles.

[632] *Cf. supra* § 1.1. This draft also assumes that the state code specifies that violating a traffic law constitutes a punishable offense. *See, e.g.*, Uniform Veh. Code § 11-102(a) ("It is unlawful, and unless otherwise declared in this chapter with respect to particular offenses, it is a (misdemeanor) (violation) for any person to do any act forbidden or fail to perform any act required in this chapter."). If the state code does not contain such language, particular offenses corresponding to provisions in this draft should also be defined.

[633] *See supra* part 6.3.3.

[634] *See, e.g., supra* part 6.2.2.

[635] *See, e.g., supra* part 6.2.2. This exception applies only if the vehicle has a virtual driver.

[636] *See, e.g., supra* part 6.2.2. This exception applies only if the vehicle has a virtual driver.

[637] *See infra* part 8. This exception applies only if the vehicle has a virtual driver.

[638] Under this provision, certain persons who are not operating an automated vehicle might nonetheless commit reckless driving. References to other vehicular crimes, such as vehicular homicide, may also be appropriate. *Cf. also supra* § 3.9.5.

[639] This language restates a common statutory provision. *See supra* part 6.3.1. It provides a basis to remove unsafe vehicles from a highway, regardless of where or if they are registered.

[640] The application of existing traffic laws to automated vehicle users could produce certain anomalous results, particularly in the absence of a virtual driver. This provision establishes a minimum level of culpability for certain offenses, some of which may be specified in other titles.

[641] *See supra* note 640.

[642] A person who can prevent a foreseeable injury should not fail to do so simply because she is not the legal driver of her vehicle.

[643] Bryant Walker Smith, *Automated Driving: State Model Bill*, cyberlaw.stanford.edu/wiki/index.php/Automated_Driving:_State_Mo del_Bill.

[644] *See supra* note 12.

[645] Geneva Convention, *supra* note 50, art. 8. The division and spacing of convoys is not required in "regions where migration of nomads occurs." *Id.* The Convention would only impede platoons if they are treated as "combination[s] of vehicles proceeding as a unit." Such combinations "may be composed of a drawing vehicle and one or two trailers," *id.* annex 6 at IV(a) and must have a driver, *id.* art. 8. "An articulated vehicle may draw a trailer, but if such articulated vehicle is used for the carriage of passengers, the trailer shall have not more than one axle and shall not carry passengers." *Id.* annex 6 at IV(a). "Any Contracting State may, however, indicate that it will only permit that one trailer be drawn by a vehicle and that it will not permit an articulated vehicle to draw a trailer. It may also indicate that it will not permit articulated vehicles for the transport of passengers." *Id.* annex 6 at IV(b).

[646] *See supra* part 5.

[647] *See supra* part 6.

[648] Other statutes may also be marginally relevant. *See, e.g.,* Cal. Veh. Code § 21711 ("No person shall operate a train of vehicles

when any vehicle being towed whips or swerves from side to side or fails to follow substantially in the path of the towing vehicle.").

[649] Uniform Veh. Code § 1-215; *see also, e.g.*, Cal. Veh. Code § 670 ("A 'vehicle' is a device by which any person or property may be propelled, moved, or drawn upon a highway, excepting a device moved exclusively by human power or used exclusively upon stationary rails or tracks.").

[650] Uniform Veh. Code §§ 1-192, 1-209, 1-213; *see also supra* note 401.

[651] *See supra* note 304; *see also* Joseph Bassano, et al., 60 C.J.S. Motor Vehicles § 12.

[652] *See supra* note 277; *cf. also* Cal. Veh. Code § 305 ("The term 'driver' does not include the tillerman or other person who, in an auxiliary capacity, assists the driver in the steering or operation of any articulated firefighting apparatus.").

[653] *See supra* part 6.1.1.

[654] *Cf. supra* part 6.1.4.

[655] *See, e.g., Partners conclude after the SARTRE project: Platooned traffic can be integrated with other road users on conventional highways*, Press Release, Sept. 17, 2012, www.sartre-project.eu/en/press/Documents/SARTRE%20final%20partner%20rel ease.pdf (minimum of four meters); Sadayuki Tsugawa, *Energy ITS: What We Learned and What We Should Learn*, 2012 Road Vehicle Automation Workshop, Transportation Research Board, July 25, 2012, onlinepubs.trb.org/onlinepubs/conferences/2012/Automation/present ations/Tsugawa.pdf (minimum of four meters); Adrian Zlocki, *KONVOI and interactIVe: Truck Platooning and Crash Avoidance*, 2012 Road Vehicle Automation Workshop, Transportation Research Board, July 25, 2012, onlinepubs.trb.org/onlinepubs/conferences/2012/Automation/present ations/Zlocki.pdf (minimum of ten meters); Steven E. Shladover, *PATH Progress on Truck Platoons and Bus Steering Guidance*, 2012 Road Vehicle Automation Workshop, Transportation Research Board, July 25, 2012, onlinepubs.trb.org/onlinepubs/conferences/2012/Automation/present ations/Shladover3.pdf (minimum of three meters).

[656] *See, e.g.*, Uniform Veh. Code § 11-310; Cal. Veh. Code §§ 21703-05; Tex. Transp. Code § 545.062; N.Y. Veh. & Traf. Law § 1129; 625 Ill. Comp. Stat. 5/11-710; 75 Pa. Cons. Stat. § 3310; Ohio Rev. Code § 4511.34; Mich. Comp. Laws § 257.643, 257.643a; Ga.

25

Code § 40-6-49; N.C. Gen. Stat. § 20-152; N.J. Stat. § 39:4-89; Va. Code § 46.2-816; Wash. Rev. Code § 46.61.145; Ind. Code §§ 9-21-8-14 - 16; Ariz. Rev. Stat. § 28-730; Tenn. Code § 55-8-124; Mo. Rev. Stat. §§ 304.017, 304.044; Md. Code Transp. § 21-310; Wis. Stat. § 346.14; Minn. Stat. § 169.18; Colo. Rev. Stat. § 42-4-1008; Ala. Code § 32-5A-89; S.C. Code § 56-5-1930; La. Rev. Stat. § 32:81; Or. Rev. Stat. § 811.485; Okla. Stat. tit. 47, § 11-310; P.R. Laws tit. 27, § 5290; Conn. Gen. Stat. §§ 14-240, 14-240a; Iowa Code §§ 321.307, 321.308; Miss. Code § 63-3-619; Ark. Code § 27-51-305; Kan. Stat. § 8-1523; Utah Code § 41-6a-711; Nev. Rev. Stat. § 484B.127; N.M. Stat. § 66-7-318; W. Va. Code § 17C-7-10; Idaho Code § 49-638; Haw. Rev. Stat. § 291C-50; Me. Rev. Stat. tit. 29-a, § 2066; N.H. Rev. Stat. § 265:25; R.I. Gen. Laws § 31-15-12; Mont. Code § 61-8-329; Del. Code tit. 21, § 4123; S.D. Codified Laws §§ 32-26-40 - 42; Alaska Admin. Code tit. 13, § 02.090; N.D. Cent. Code § 39-10-18; Vt. Stat. tit. 23, § 1039; D.C. Code § 18 DC ADC 2201; Wyo. Stat. § 31-5-210; Guam Code tit. 16, § 3320; Navajo Nation Code tit. 14, § 306; *see generally* J. H. Cooper, *Driver's failure to maintain proper distance from motor vehicle ahead*, 85 A.L.R.2d 613.

[657] *See, e.g., Ratliff v. Duke Power Co.*, 151 S.E.2d 641, 268 N.C. 605 (N.C. 1966); Cooper, *supra* note 656.

[658] *E.g.*, Uniform Veh. Code § 11-310(a); Cal. Veh. Code § 21703; N.Y. Veh. & Traf. Law § 1129(a); Fla. Stat. § 316.0895(a); 625 Ill. Comp. Stat. 5/11-710(a); *cf.* Tex. Transp. Code § 545.062(a) ("An operator shall, if following another vehicle, maintain an assured clear distance between the two vehicles so that, considering the speed of the vehicles, traffic, and the conditions of the highway, the operator can safely stop without colliding with the preceding vehicle or veering into another vehicle, object, or person on or near the highway.").

[659] *See supra* part 6.3.3. Alabama additionally provides that "[e]xcept when overtaking and passing another vehicle, the driver of a vehicle shall leave a distance of at least 20 feet for each 10 miles per hour of speed between the vehicle that he or she is driving and the vehicle that he or she is following." Ala. Code § 32-5A-89(a).

[660] Uniform Veh. Code § 11-310(b), (c).

[661] *See, e.g.*, Cal. Veh. Code § 21704; Tex. Transp. Code § 545.062(b); N.Y. Veh. & Traf. Law § 1129(b); Fla. Stat. § 316.0895(2); 625 Ill. Comp. Stat. 5/11-710(b). These provisions generally do not prohibit "overtaking and passing" by such vehicles. Uniform Veh. Code § 11-310(b).

[662] Fla. Stat. § 316.0895(4); Ohio Rev. Code § 4511.34(A); Minn. Stat. § 169.18(b); Iowa Code § 321.308; Miss. Code § 63-3-619(2); W. Va. Code § 17C-7-10(b) (additionally excluding military convoys).

[663] Cal. Veh. Code § 21704 (300 feet); Fla. Stat. § 316.0895(4) (300 feet); Mich. Comp. Laws § 257.643 (500 feet); N.J. Stat. § 39:4-89 (100 feet); Tenn. Code § 55-8-124(d) (300 feet); Mo. Rev. Stat. § 304.044 (300 feet); Wis. Stat. § 346.14 (500 feet); Minn. Stat. § 169.18(b) (500 feet); Ala. Code § 32-5A-89(b) (300 feet); La. Rev. Stat. § 32:81(B) (400 feet); Okla. Stat. tit. 47, § 11-310 (300 feet); Iowa Code § 321.308 (300 feet); Ark. Code § 27-51-305(b) (200 feet); Nev. Rev. Stat. § 484B.127(2) (500 feet); N.M. Stat. § 66-7-318(B) (300 feet); W. Va. Code § 17C-7-10(b) (200 feet); Me. Rev. Stat. tit. 29-a, § 2066(4) (150 feet).

[664] Uniform Veh. Code § 11-310(c). Caravan and motorcade are not defined.

[665] Cal. Veh. Code § 21705 (100 feet); Okla. Stat. tit. 47, § 11-310(d) (200 feet); N.M. Stat. § 66-7-318(C) (300 feet).

[666] See, e.g., supra part 6.5 § 7.6.

www.ingramcontent.com/pod-product-compliance
Lightning Source LLC
Chambersburg PA
CBHW051516170526
45165CB00002B/497